On Tolkien, His world, and a
Better Understanding of Ours

Letters
from
the
Shire

Matthew J. Distefano

All rights reserved. No part of this book may be used or reproduced, stored in a retrieval system, or transmitted in any form or by any means, electronic, mechanical, photocopying, recording, scanning, or otherwise, without written permission from the publisher except in the case of brief quotations embodied in critical articles and reviews. Permission for wider usage of this material can be obtained through Quoir by emailing permission@quoir.com.

Copyright © 2025 by Matthew J. Distefano

First Edition

Scripture quotations are taken from the New Revised Standard Version Updated Edition. Copyright © 2021 National Council of Churches of Christ in the United States of America. Used by permission. All rights reserved worldwide.

Cover Design & Interior Layout by Matthew J. Distefano
Cover Image by Keith Giles

ISBN 978-1-964252-49-0

Printed in the United States of America

Published by Quoir
Chico, California
www.quoir.com

Letters

Dedicated to Lyndsay and Elyse, Michael and Speri,
and everyone who loves Middle-earth

PREFACE

September 22 has, for years, held a special place in my heart. Not only is it the birthday of Bilbo and Frodo Baggins—two of the most famous Hobbits in the history of Middle-earth—but it marks the beginning of one of the greatest adventures ever told. Fittingly, then, I chose to complete this collection of letters around that date. But rather than releasing it on the 22nd itself, I've opted for September 23—the day Frodo leaves the Shire.

This choice feels fitting. While birthdays celebrate beginnings, the day after is where the real journey begins. That's when the packing's done, the map's in hand, and the road is stretching out before you, unexpected and uncertain. And that's where this book finds us—not in the cozy safety of Bag End, but on the cusp of the unknown.

The following letters are part of an ongoing adventure I've been on for many years now, one that's seen its share of laughter, pipe-weed, late-night conversations around the bonfire, and quiet mornings among the tomatoes and herbs at Happy Woods Farm. But more than anything, this journey has been marked by friendship.

When I first began writing about Tolkien—starting with *The Wisdom of Hobbits* and continuing with *Mimetic Theory & Middle-earth*—I didn't just want to analyze the stories academically or treat Middle-earth like a mere text to be dissected. I wanted to live with it, breathe with it, walk through its fields with bare feet. And I wanted to do so alongside others.

That's why this book exists.

Letters from the Shire is a conversation—a long, meandering, pipe-weed infused kind of chat—with people I care about. Some are dear friends and colleagues. Others are readers whose curiosity and thoughtful questions have challenged me in the best ways. All of them helped shape the reflections in these pages.

This is also a deeply *mimetic* book, in the most positive and hopeful sense of the word. When we talk about mimesis, especially in the Girardian tradition, we're often focused on the dangers of imitation—how rivalry, resentment, and retribution spiral out of control when we imitate the wrong models. But imitation can also be a beautiful, life-giving thing. And in this case, I wanted to model my own work after that of J.R.R. Tolkien himself.

If you've ever picked up *The Letters of J.R.R. Tolkien*, you'll know what I mean. The book is a treasure trove of relational and creative insight. In his letters to family, friends, publishers, and fans, we find not just a glimpse into the mind of a master myth-maker, but a man who thought deeply, felt tenderly, and cared immensely about what he spent his life painstakingly creating. His letters are full of clarity, wit, theological depth, and even humor. I can't claim to match the Professor's wisdom, but I wanted to try writing in the same spirit—with honesty, affection, curiosity, and a touch of smoke from the firepit and the pipe.

Following this collection of letters, I include two short writings that respond to reviews of *The Wisdom of Hobbits* and *Mimetic Theory & Middle-earth*. I've always believed writing should be a dialogue, not a monologue, and sometimes the best insights come not from my own pen, but from the poking and prodding of others. Whether a reader was praising the text or pushing back against something I'd written, I wanted to offer a thoughtful reply.

And yes, for those who've been following the work I do at Happy Woods Farm, I'll also be sharing an update on our little slice of Hobbiton heaven. Since the publication of those earlier books, life on our land has continued to shape and teach me. There's something about adding yet more compost to the garden beds or watching the chickens scratch at the ground that keeps my thoughts rooted—pun intended—and reminds me of the sacredness of the simple things.

Now, before you journey on into the letters themselves, I need to take a moment to honor two people whose absence I feel profoundly.

First, my friend Jim Wehde, who asked one of the questions included in this book and attended *The Wisdom of Hobbits* launch party at my home in Chico. Jim passed away in early 2025, and his absence is still fresh in my heart. He was the kind of friend who made you feel seen, who asked questions not to impress, but to understand. He read deeply, listened well, and always had something thoughtful to offer our conversations. His passing saddened me, and I dedicate this collection in part to his memory.

Second, I want to recognize Amanda Drake from *The Tolkien Society*, who wrote one of the earliest and most generous reviews of *The Wisdom of Hobbits*. Amanda's insight and encouragement meant more to me than I probably ever adequately expressed. Her passing this year came as a shock to many of us, and her light, both as a scholar and a soul, will be missed.

If there's one thing Middle-earth teaches us, it's that all good journeys are forged in fellowship, and that no road should be walked alone. These letters, then, are my offering of fellowship to you. I hope they make you think. I hope they make you smile. And I hope they remind you—whether you're in a Hobbit hole, a big city, or somewhere in between—that you are never truly alone when you walk with friends.

— **Matthew J. Distefano**
March 6, 2025
Chico, California

Acknowledgments

No book is ever written alone, and this one—perhaps more than any other—has been shaped by others who helped form these pages.

First, to my wife, Lyndsay: thank you for your patience, encouragement, and constant grounding presence. And to my daughter Elyse, who reminds me every day what real bravery looks like.

To Keith Giles, my business partner at Quoir and fellow heretic at *Heretic Happy Hour*: thank you for continuing to believe in the work we are doing.

To my best friend Michael Machuga: what can I say at this point? Just that I hope we get to live on the same street someday.

To everyone who contributed a question for these letters, thank you for inviting me into meaningful conversation. Your curiosity spawned some fantastic musings.

To Andy Colenzo, Sarah and Jordan Mallory, Speri Machuga, and Michelle Collins, for your friendship.

To Dave and Sharon Wohnoutka, for parenting someone as complicated as your very tall Hobbit son.

To Crystal Kuld, for being a fantastic editor whose finesse and creativity help refine my more rougherest edges.

To Nick Polk and everyone at *The Tolkien Society*, thank you for your dedication to preserving and deepening the legacy of the Professor. It's an honor to walk among such devoted stewards of his world.

And finally, to every single person who reads my books, you are part of this fellowship now. May your road rise to meet you, your garden always grow well, and your heart stay open to the small and simple things in life.

One

On Literature

"What is it about The Lord of the Rings *that continues to inspire and fascinate people today? What sets it apart from typical 'sword and sorcery' literature?"*

— **Keith Giles**

Dear Keith,

How many fantasy books have included wizards, elves, dwarves, magic, enchantments, and sorcery? Don't answer or you'll be up counting all night! Maybe it's because I'm a publisher who learned design from one of the greats, but I cringe as I picture all those recycled book covers featuring fire-breathing dragons jumping off the page and scantily-clad Elven heroes only kept at bay by some Cinzel Decorative-type font one and a half times the necessary size. No offense to anyone who has used such a formula for their fantasy series, but it's a bit played out, don't you think?

That's not to say there are no great stories following an already tried-and-true formula. There are. I'm not here to disrespect anyone. But what J.R.R. Tolkien has done with not only *The Lord of the Rings*, but his entire Legendarium, is second to none in scope and size, and uniquely developed compared to most fantasy literature that has followed since.

This may sound shocking, but I don't think of Tolkien *primarily* as the author of *The Lord of the Rings*. Rather, I think of him as a world-builder and myth-maker whose most famous tale undoubtedly belongs front and center within the history of his world, but only as a part of the larger whole. While other fantasy authors world-build, none do it quite as well as the Good Professor.

So, that's the first reason we are still enamored with Middle-earth—Tolkien's world building is only matched in greatness by the mushrooms on Maggot's farm (if you don't get that joke, it's okay, I'll forgive you). But this is not the only reason. Tolkien also understood the polar extremes of the human experience, both phenomenologically and spiritually. His *characters* deeply resonate with us. We see ourselves in them because we *are* them. Some of us are bashful gardeners, too shy to ask that cute girl on a date. Others are impulsive and somewhat immature, but ultimately, and perhaps unfairly, misunderstood. Some become too wounded for home to ever feel like home again. Yet others—no one stumbling upon these letters, of course—have been so corrupted by greed and power that they have long since become shadows of their former selves.

How many people do we know who have been so corrupted like this? And how true is it that when we stop to *really* think about their particular life circumstances, we can't help but pity them? I've known a lot of people I could categorize as Gollum-like, so I know where Bilbo and Frodo are coming from when *they* can't help but pity the creature formerly known as Sméagol.

Sméagol *is* a Hobbit, after all—perhaps a malicious Hobbit, but a Hobbit nonetheless—so any fellow halfling with even a skosh of honest reflection is going to end up seeing at least a part of themselves in the wretched trickster, no matter how treacherous he has become. The always wise Gandalf reminds us that there are indeed Hobbit-friends of *his* who could have ended up just as corrupted by the Ring, which is partly why he rejects it when offered.[1] Toward the end of *The Return of the King*, Frodo even acknowledges the following to Sam:

> "Do you remember Gandalf's words: Even Gollum may have something yet to do? But for him, Sam, I could not have destroyed the Ring. The Quest would have been in vain, even at the bitter end. So let us forgive him! For the Quest is achieved, and now all is over."[2]

Forgiveness is an interesting choice of words here. It's almost as if Frodo instantly realizes two things at the same time: 1) just how corrupted by the Ring he has become, and 2) that had Gollum not been there on the precipice of the Cracks of Doom, he would have walked back down the mountain with it, becoming the very thing he claimed to hate. So, in a very real way, Frodo *understands*

Gollum's plight the minute he has this revelation about *himself* and his corruptible nature.

Okay, so where have I been going with all this?

My meanderings only goes to show just how multi-faceted and well thought-out Tolkien's world really is. You asked what sets *The Lord of the Rings* apart from run-of-the-mill fantasy literature, and I'm off getting distracted by the resoundingly deep character development of the so-called Manichean "bad guys" from a story written nearly a century ago.[3]

Point, Tolkien.

Longevity like this is about more than just interesting characters, however; it's about having characters that develop (or regress) *in the same way we do.* The personalities must be believable, even if they live and move and have their being in an unbelievable world—one replete with dragons, shapeshifters, balrogs, and Ents (and their wives, if they can ever find them!). As Michael [Machuga] has commented in a private conversation around our firepit: "I don't particularly care what Frodo and Sam are doing; I care about *them.*"

Don't get it twisted: the plot of *The Lord of the Rings* is not a complicated one. *An unsung hero has to make a journey from his humble home to some scary land, and the fate of the world depends on it.* We've heard this story a million times. So, what makes *this* particular hero's journey one we are still spilling ink over so many years later? Allow me to repeat myself: First, the entire mythology is built in such a way that if it ever becomes discovered by extraterrestrials long after humanity's inevitable collapse, they'll never believe it was created by one man and not over millennia. Second, the characters are so well developed, lovable (even when we hate them), and believable, that we can't help but return to their stories, year after year, in print, on the screen, and even with video-game controllers in our hands (though I'm still waiting for a decent adaptation for the current gen systems).

These two explanations for the mythology's longevity are only a part of the entire picture one would have to paint to do justice to Tolkien and his Legendarium, however. I haven't even started mentioning all the Professor has offered the world of theology, philosophy, ecology, politics, and perhaps most importantly, the growing and smoking of pipe-weed. You know, *the real important topics for a well-lived life!*

That's what Hobbits would have us believe, anyway. And perhaps they are right. When you smoke from a pipe, you slow down and become more *present.* When I smoke from mine, I like to look over the garden Michael and I have cultivated over the course of our long friendship, which only brings me closer to what Fr. Richard Rohr calls "the naked now." Given the emphasis toward such themes in Tolkien's works, it's safe to say he was certainly onto something with his Hobbits and their love of pipe-weed. Being present *is* an art, just as it is known in the Shire. Any process of slowing down is. To be still, and present, and here and now, takes practice. You don't get proficient at the piano, for instance, just by listening to Chopin; the art moves through you as you practice and practice. And in your practicing, you learn to be present with your form.

So, yeah, Tolkien understood what it means to be human, and that's one reason why we still care.

Yours.

---

1. Tolkien, *The Fellowship of the Ring*, 59.

2. Tolkien, *The Return of the King*, 241.

3. Part of the genius of Tolkien is that he doesn't give us Manichean good and bad guys. Gollum is complex, and is never beyond redemption (though it *is* a fool's hope). And Frodo, well, his goodness isn't enough to overcome the lure of the Ring at the eleventh hour, though I would still contend he is indeed "good."

Two

ON CULTURAL RELEVANCE

"The Lord of the Rings was published in the 1950s. Our society has undergone many changes since then, including the civil rights movement, changes in how we understand gender, the legalization of gay marriage, and the creation of the internet. Considering how different our world is today, as compared to the world in which J.R.R. Tolkien lived and wrote, would The Lord of the Rings *still be published in the twenty-first century?"*

— **Kayla Kaml-Decker**

Dear Kayla,

Our society has indeed undergone many changes. I wonder, though: are we really *all that* different from folks back in Tolkien's day? Even if our generations are as disparate as a long-bearded Dwarf and a platinum-haired Elf, we all know that *some* works of art transcend generations. *The Lord of the Rings* is certainly one of these.

Wouldn't you agree?

Of course, there may be *some* publishers in today's world who would not want to publish a book like *The Lord of the Rings*, but much of the worry about so-called "cancel culture" is overblown and unrealistic, if that's what you're getting at. Sure, the Right will have us believe that if you sneeze wrongly in front of a liberal, you'll have your social media presence scrubbed before being blacklisted by every "woke" company in your local "sanctuary city." But let's be honest: Chris Pratt still works in Hollywood, Joe Rogan still has a nine-figure Spotify contract, and Dave Chappelle still puts out Netflix specials, so I think we can all just relax for a second.

Moreover, *The Lord of the Rings* only gets more and more popular, so something tells me people today are still craving good storytelling and thoughtful character development, which "LOTR" provides in droves.

That being said, if Tolkien's heyday were today, rather than three quarters of a century ago, I would think that his stories might look slightly different than compared to their 1950s form. That's just how personal context works. None of us can approach the world tabula rasa—*with a clean slate*—and we will always create through our own subjective lenses.

Tolkien included.

Does that mean his stories would be *dramatically* different if written nowadays? Not necessarily. Perhaps they would only be slightly altered—but they *would* be altered. The only question is *how?* Would Tolkien be cognizant of the importance of racial representation within literature? Would he include an explicitly LGBTQ+ character? How about a Black Hobbit? There's no way to know, but it's fun to imagine; because if we think Ted Sandyman (the Shire's version of Tucker Carlson) was prejudice before, imagine a Black Hobbit from Michel Delving strolling into *The Ivy Bush*!

At the end of the day, however, I'm convinced *The Lord of the Rings* would certainly exist today. Genius is genius, and our current society can spot brilliance.

Then again, the real Tolkien should have died with all his friends in WWI, so maybe the current iteration of *The Lord of the Rings* is a miracle unto itself. Perhaps in every other version of the multiverse, the Good Professor gets cut down way too young. That's what happened to his friend Geoffrey Bache Smith, the poet who never was, as well as two of his fellow Exeter College mates, Max Windle and Osric Staples. Without war, who would these men have become? We'll never know, which is why we should cherish artists like Tolkien.

Now that I think of it, perhaps this is one reason why Tolkien was so anti-war. He had tasted it first-hand and discovered no glory there, only suffering. Even when it is a necessary evil throughout his Legendarium, the best leaders employ war as a *truly* last resort, and often just to distract the enemy. Think about the Battle of the Morannon from *The Return of the King*. Aragorn marches to meet Sauron's forces outside the Black Gate, knowing full well he and his army cannot prevail in battle. They are merely there to distract Sauron long enough for Frodo and Sam to finish the Quest of the Ring, a secret mission in which the heroes commit no violence, their only sacrifices being of the *self*.

Is this not precisely the type of story we need in today's world? I believe it is, and I believe there would be a place for Tolkien to create it, even if he had been born in 1992 rather than 1892. War is war and having literature that doesn't place it on any kind of pedestal is always a welcome addition to a society's shared collection.

At least, that's how we feel at Quoir Publishing. So, if the version of HarperCollins in the multiverse where Tolkien publishes in 2024 rather than 1954 decides they want to pass on his little story, I guess Quoir could give it a shot. And I guess that means the short answer to your question is "yes." At minimum, I co-own a publishing house and would jump at the idea of publishing *The Lord of the Rings*. In 2044, it will go into the public domain here in the United States; so, given our company has an imprint called Quoir Classics, I suppose I will be able to. What an oddly surreal day that will be!

Yours.

Three

On Challenging the Status Quo

"With The Lord of the Rings *being timeless literature, what events did it speak to when J.R.R. Tolkien first wrote the stories? And what events does it speak to today? What status quos does the book challenge? In what ways might the story inspire readers to live differently and create change?"*

— Glenn Siepert

Dear Glenn,

There is nothing like a four-part question to get the blood pumping! But what a fun opportunity to dive into some challenging ideas and potential real-world applications for some of the concepts from Tolkien's world.

First off, it's difficult to not notice the influence World War I had on Tolkien. As a Brit, he was deployed to France, witnessed the death of his friends, came down with "trench fever,"[1] and was shipped back home to recover. Incidentally, this discharge from the war likely saved Tolkien's life, as he was never sent back to the front lines.

I mention this at the onset because, while war and violence are prevalent throughout *The Lord of the Rings*, neither are championed. War is portrayed for what it is—a purveyor of darkness and destruction. We mourn the deaths of Boromir, King Théoden (and his horse Snowmane), Théodred, Beechbone the Ent, Denethor (kinda), and even Lotho Sackville-Baggins, but only after the "confounded" Hobbit is alleged to have been eaten by Grima Wormtongue during the events of the War of the Ring (forked-tongue, indeed!). Even when we attain a sense of victory through battle, it always comes at a heavy cost.

How relevant to our world today!

As it currently stands, there are conflicts occurring in just about every continent. In the West, instability and violence in Haiti, Mexico, and Venezuela are everyday occurrences. Civil wars are playing out in the African countries of Libya, Sudan, and Central African Republic. We all know about the violence in Yemen, Israel, Gaza, Lebanon, Turkey, and Syria, as well as the ongoing tensions between India and Pakistan. And let's not forget the war in Ukraine, the civil war in Myanmar, the territorial disputes in the South China Sea, the confrontation over Taiwan, and whatever the hell continues to goes on up in North Korea. Oh, and I need not even mention the daily incidences of gun violence in the US, or how our government recently sent in the military to Los Angeles to quell the protests against the inhumane ICE. Just about everywhere we turn, "wars and rumors of war"[2]—to quote the Bible—are commonplace.

So, how does Tolkien challenge this status-quo approach to conflict resolution? In a multitude of ways. In a January 14 letter to Kayla Kaml-Decker, I mention how, during the events of *The Lord of the Rings*, war is initiated by the Free People of Middle-earth *only* for the goal of distracting the enemy. When war is brought to the doorstep of Helm's Deep and Minas Tirith, the people fight (and for good reason!); but war is never used as a tool for gaining *anything*. It is always wrought with loss, even in victory.

True, long-lasting triumph, however, is not won through force. In fact, as I discuss in *The Wisdom of Hobbits*, good never actually forcefully abolishes evil. Instead, evil destroys itself—it is designed that way. The Ring, for example, can only be destroyed *where*? In Mordor. And where is Sauron? In Mordor. And what is he actively doing at all times and in all places? Looking for the Ring and attempting to lure it to Mordor. And what is the Ring doing throughout this time? Luring its host to the one place it needs to go, but is also the one place it risks being destroyed—you guessed it... Mordor! And even when the Ring is lost to the fires below, it isn't because goodness triumphs. No! Gollum takes possession of the Ring before falling in along with it, which I would say is quite poetic—I'm just not sure if it is catastrophic or eucatastrophic (given my pity for Gollum).

This is why we must find new solutions to old problems: our old solutions simply aren't working. As a species, we continually engage in the very endeavors that perpetuates the problem in the first place, attempting to be the all-powerful Manichean "good guy" who defeats the just-as-powerful Manichean "bad guy." In doing so, we quell out-and-out violence with mediated violence (or so we tell ourselves). While this sort of "works" for a time and to a degree, such an approach only serves to kick the can down the road. After all, violence begets violence, and no one thinks their violence is the bad kind.

The heroes of Middle-earth often employ a different approach, however.

Take Samwise, for instance—humble, works with his hands, lives a life many of us can relate to. But even Sam has his passions and desires, and thus, his potential weaknesses. Near the tower of Cirith Ungol, the Ring discovers what these passions/desires are, and attempts to make an in road into his psyche. Here's Tolkien, describing that event:

> As Sam stood there, even though the Ring was not on him but hanging by its chain about his neck, he felt himself enlarged, as if he were robed in a huge distorted shadow of himself, a vast and ominous threat halted upon the walls of Mordor. He felt that he had from now on only two choices, to forbear the Ring, though it would torment him; or to claim it, and challenge the Power that sat in its dark hold beyond the valley of shadows. Already the Ring tempted him, gnawing at his will and reason. Wild fantasies arose in his mind; and he saw Samwise the Strong, Hero of the Age, striding with a flaming sword across the darkened land, and armies flocking to his call as he marched to the overthrow of Barad-dur. And then all the clouds rolled away, and the white sun shone, and at his command the vale of Gorgoroth became a garden of flowers and trees and brought forth fruit. He had only to put on the Ring and claim it for his own, and all this could be.[3]

For a gardener like Sam, this is a great temptation, perhaps greater than any he could fathom. And yet, the Ring is not Sam's model—Frodo is. So the ever-diligent and surprisingly wise Hobbit rejects its bid. Tolkien continues:

> In that hour of trial it was his love of his master that helped most to hold him firm; but also deep down in him lived still unconquered his plain hobbit-sense: he knew in the core of his heart that he was not large enough to bear such a burden, even if such visions were not a mere cheat to betray him. The one small garden of a free gardener was all his need and due, not a garden swollen to a realm; his own hands to use, not the hands of others to command.[4]

This is where *true power* originates from—in friendship, and in humility. Even when faced with a desire for perceived power, friendship, if at the forefront of our conscious minds, can always motivate and bring out the best in us. That's exactly what his closeness to Frodo does for Sam, whose loyalty to his friend is even stronger than his desire to lord over the greatest garden in all of Middle-earth—something no good gardener even dreams of, as Sam rightly admits.

So, to answer your last question: how can this knowledge create change in *our* world? In *Mimetic Theory & Middle-earth*, I argue that it can alter our course in profound ways. My contention is that if we are all more conscious about those we take on as models, the world will experience a type of healing not yet seen in history. The problem is that so much of our mimetic nature is below the line of *conscious awareness*.

But is discovering change as simple as *being aware*? No... awareness is a crucially foundational piece of the puzzle though. Other key ingredients are needed, many of which can be found throughout Tolkien's Legendarium. The question, then, becomes, *will we both heed its warnings and apply its teachings?* Time will tell, but as his works gain more and more popularity, I gain more and more confidence we'll get there someday.

Yours.

---

1. Trench fever is a bacterial infection caused by Bartonella quintana. It is characterized by fever, headache, and shin pain, and was prevalent during WWI.

2. See Matthew 24:6–13.

3. Tolkien, *The Return of the King*, 185–86.

4. Ibid., 186.

Four

ON THE THERAPEUTIC QUALITIES OF NATURE

"I can't even look at the huge gingko biloba trees outside our home without noticing how they interact with each other, with us, with the environment. Part of this awareness is due, in part, to J.R.R. Tolkien. With his particular style of prose, could it be that the Professor is trying to get us to see our Creator all throughout nature? Is this also why growing these things becomes so therapeutic for us?"

— **Denis Tate**

Dear Denis,

Like you, I cannot help but notice the interconnectedness of everything around us. I view my fruit trees with the same fondness most people give their dogs. Last year, one of our cherries got a leaf fungus, and it legit stressed me out. Thank Eru for modern solutions

17

like fungicidal sprays! They have saved many a tree, not to mention last year's blackberry crop.

When fungi and parasites aren't trying to destroy hard-earned crops—or, worse yet, all of humanity like in *The Last of Us*—gardening is quite the therapy, isn't it? I take in many moments throughout the week, soaking in the naked now as often as I'm able. It's always after smoking from my pipe, which is why I continually assert that I am a Hobbit in all but size.

But back to fungi and parasites...

Are these, too, not a part of Arda? Do they not belong in the kingdom of God? Any true Hobbit would place mushrooms at the top of the list of life's pleasures, but aren't mushrooms a type of fungus, too? All I'm saying is that even the so-called problems of life (leaf fungi included) aren't *necessarily* problems. Our cherry tree didn't die—neither did our blackberries—and spraying crops can actually be quite therapeutic, if you allow it to be. That's why you see all those Buddhist monks sweeping stairs for hours on end. It's also why people would travel—literally *travel*—to watch Brother Lawrence peel *po-ta-toes*. Focused on the present moment, "tasks" such as this can become quite a sacred experience.

The "mundane" aspects of life are also verifiably secular as well. Sweeping steps. Spraying fruit trees. Peeling potatoes. These are all "earthy" in nature. Most work with our hands is. But if you allow yourself to slide into the present moment, you can find oneness with God, no matter the task.

At this point, some may be moved to call me new-agey, but 1) *no*, and 2) there's a long history of thought development here. Given how Tolkien was a devout Catholic, I'm reminded of the

Franciscans, who emphasize creation and the natural world above all other theological matters. Why? Because nature is where you find God. Quite literally. In *Canticle of the Creatures*, St. Francis expresses profound fondness towards animals and even inanimate objects, viewing them as co-inhabitants of Creation. Fr. Richard Rohr says that, "nature is the one song of praise that never stops singing."[1] And though not a Franciscan, but certainly a Catholic, Thomas Aquinas once wrote, "Creation is the primary and most perfect revelation of the Divine."[2]

Protestants, by and large, have lost sight of this reverence for the natural world. In my estimations, they've lost sight of a lot of things, but this is neither the time nor the place for a rant about Protestantism. I'm certainly no Catholic, but I do appreciate the veneration for nature this tradition holds.

Hobbits, on the other hand, have no formal religion at all. Instead, they have an almost magical kinship with the earth, allowing them to even disappear into the landscape if need be.

So, it's an interesting observation: Tolkien was a devout Catholic, but when he envisioned the most idyllic culture, he came up with the completely secular Hobbit.

Again, though, there is no such sacred/secular divide. Both Hobbits and Franciscans know this. But wait, didn't I just say that Hobbits are non-religious? Yes, but being religious is not the same thing as acknowledging the sacred. I'm sure certain Hobbits believe in Ilúvatar, even if they don't worship him or perform any ritualistic rites in his honor. While Hobbits certainly *are* ritualistic—as all cultures are—none of their practices are directly related to Eru or any of the pantheon (the Valar).

Yet another reason I am a Hobbit in all but size...

When I surround myself in nature, I don't think of the word G-O-D. That term no longer has any use for me, as it comes with too many theological assumptions. This is especially true here in the States, where the toxic Religious Right have all but hijacked Christianity. But for me, when I'm gardening, it's simply an exercise in *presence* with the plants, with the soil, with the water, with the sun, with the clouds passing overhead, with the butterflies and dragonflies flittering across the lawn, with the chickens clucking in their run, and with my best friend Michael there alongside me.

Because here's the rub: we have to have community and fellowship, along with nature. Even we introverts need *some* kind of connection. It may take us a few days to recover after hanging out with you, but we'll eventually be back for more camaraderie, assuming you, too, are a good and decent Hobbit.

In parting, I consider you to be one of these. So, until we meet face to face, be well, and keep enjoying your gingko trees.

Yours.

---

1. See https://cac.org/daily-meditations/nature-first-bible-weekly-summary-2015-01-24/.

2. Ibid.

Five

ON FEMINISM

*"Would you classify J.R.R. Tolkien as a feminist?
Galadriel is arguably the most powerful female character
in Middle-earth, yet female characters occur only briefly
throughout Tolkien's works. And is Éowyn a shamanic,
feminist icon born of Tolkien's own childhood experiences,
or simply a medieval maternalist, meant to prescribe
women a more traditional role?"*

— Meghan Irene Turner

Dear Meghan,

This is a fascinating set of questions, and similar inquiries have been asked in the past. Answers have predictably fallen all over the spectrum, given *The Lord of the Rings'* relationship to women (or lack thereof, according to critics of Tolkien).

To your first question, though: *is J.R.R. Tolkien a feminist?* By modern standards—as if culture is anywhere close to monolithic in its definition of the word—I would have to say *no*. But applying modern definitions to historical figures is, oftentimes, an exercise in futility (this is one reason Tolkien may not even be considered an "environmentalist," but that's a topic for another time).

Is Tolkien a feminist in the vaguest sense of the word, however? We can't be sure, though the Professor did seem to advocate for the rights of all people, regardless of sex; on the flipside, he also seemed to have a narrow and now-outdated view of women. Nevertheless, "feminist" is a bit of a loaded term, and carries with it a meaning that has shifted even since Tolkien's death in 1973.

That's one reason it's so difficult to assess people who grew up over 100 years prior to our current context. When we do, sometimes things feel cringey. In a 1941 letter to his son Michael, for example, Tolkien describes women as "... not much more than helpers who rely on instinct, their gift being always remaining receptive to the wills of men."

Not great, I'll admit.

If we apply this knowledge to the text and look to conclude that Tolkien was adamant about portraying Middle-earth's women as the lesser sex, we'll likely find enough evidence to support this claim. Most main characters are men, and even when women appear, their presence is brief and, according to many of Tolkien's detractors, often caricaturized.

However, dismissing Tolkien as merely a sexist, without acknowledging the historical context he was shaped by, and the fact that society has since moved on, is overly reductive. For starters,

Tolkien's female characters, rather than simply being caricatures of what "true womanhood" is allegedly supposed to look like, are quite developed in many ways. Galadriel, for instance, possesses a dark, powerful mystique that is atypical compared to what we might automatically visualize in archetypal feminine qualities. Sure, when the Fellowship enters Lothlórien after escaping from the Mines of Moria, she is described with "chaste, virginal imagery,"[1] to quote Rachel Maddox (one of Tolkien's harshest critics in this regard). The Lady of Lórien is clad in white, with light skin and hair to match, emblematic of how many Catholics envision the Virgin Mary. Again, though, to fixate on this imagery without also considering the fact that she plays a lead role—while her husband Celeborn takes a more supportive one—is to take a myopic approach. After all, as the joke goes, "If you ever feel useless, remember Galadriel has a husband."

Moreover, I can't help but notice that among Tolkien's most important takeaways is the assertion that the truly wise are those who are able to repel the desire for power. Case in point: when Galadriel is confronted by the Ring, she, like the wizard Gandalf before her, is able to resist its lure. In fact, in helping Frodo to destroy the Ring, she is giving up literally everything important to her. How? Because the power of her *own ring* is tied to the existence of the One Ring. Eliminating the latter strips the power of the former, which is the only thing keeping Lothlórien from succumbing to the natural process of entropy. That is why, after the events of the War of the Ring, Galadriel—and eventually all the Elves—leave Middle-earth for the Undying Lands. Once the rings are destroyed, they fade, as foretold by the prophecies. For Frodo and the Fellowship, she gives up all this power when she could have easily taken it, thus proving her status among the greatest of heroes.

Then there's Éowyn of Rohan—what to do with her?

Maddox seems to believe that Éowyn's story, "implies that when women break from their naturally submissive natures, there are often disastrous consequences."[2] If true, then the answer to your final question appears clear—Tolkien wrote Éowyn as a maternalistic figure, and her break from a traditionalist feminine role serves as a cautionary tale meant to make potential feminists of all kinds shudder. But does Éowyn's story end in disaster? Not by a long shot! There are consequences to her actions, no doubt, but that's true for every character we meet. In the end, however, Éowyn's story ends in bliss, with her being counted among the most heroic in all of Middle-earth. Sure, one could say that her hopelessness had once pushed her toward "deserting" her people and her king, but her acts of bravery and heroism cannot be overlooked. As Dawn Catanach notes, "Some call her [Éowyn] a heroine while others consider her a deserter. But she is not unequivocally deserving of either label. The truth of her character lies somewhere in between."[3]

Even Maddox is forced to agree, noting: "Éowyn's [...] strength in battle, psychological complexity, and participation in the typically masculine ritual of hero worship confirm that she, too, exhibits the complexity of a realistic character."[4] Like Galadriel, though, there are indeed "traditional" depictions of her femininity—her story comes from an ancient patriarchal myth, after all—but historically masculine traits are present as well, compelling even Tolkien's staunchest critics to acknowledge that there is a level of depth within his female characters.

And yet, can Tolkien's depictions also be problematic? As with any interpretation, it comes down to hermeneutics. What I mean by this is simple: if we approach any text with malice, we will find what we are looking for and can use our perception of the text to justify our own bigotry and misogyny. That's how it is with the Bible, with the Qur'an, with *The Lord of the Rings*—any myth, really. On the other hand, there's nothing preventing us from taking an entirely different approach, seeking out where we can find women being uplifted and championed. Éowyn is the killer of the Witch-king of Angmar—a truly astounding feat—not merely a figure in some cautionary tale warning women of what happens when they break traditional gender norms. And Galadriel is not just a milky-white face with stereotypically golden locks; she is perhaps the most powerful figure in all of Middle-earth's Third Age, yet remains incorruptible where lesser *men* would have failed, and in fact did (see, Boromir).

At the end of the day, people are people—we are messy and complex, and often end up looking rather silly when judged by future standards. Was Tolkien *anti*-woman? I don't think so. Did he possess views about them that we now consider outdated and problematic? This would be quite a fair assessment. The humbling thing is being aware that when history looks back and judges *us*, it may not always be too kind. That's just how progress works, which again reiterates my earlier point that we should do our best to be slow to judge the past by our present standards. What's important is that we take the best of the past, learn

25

from the worst of it, and continue carving out a world where all races, genders, sexes, and sexual orientations are celebrated and honored, rather than diminished and caricaturized. My hope is that, should Tolkien have been born 100 years later, my favorite author would agree with me—but I'll have to wait to ask him until we meet in the great beyond, at the end of all things.

Yours.

---

1. Maddox, "Flawed and Formidable," 3.

2. Ibid., 2.

3. Catanach, "The Problem of Éowyn," 1.

4. Maddox, "Flawed and Formidable," 10.

Six

ON THE ENTS

"What is nature's role in The Lord of the Rings, *and what characteristics does it possess? Given the depth of character and array of emotionality J.R.R. Tolkien gave to the Ents, what would their message to society be today if we came face to face with them?"*

— **Nikki Stoy**

Dear Nikki,

Nature plays a prominent role in Tolkien's world, in both benevolent and malicious ways. Most of us recognize all the ways the natural world *positively* impacts our favorite characters—we love how Hobbits dig their homes into the earth, and how Rivendell becomes a sanctuary for weary travelers—but the natural world can also turn on people, in the case of Old Man Willow, or even the Ents.

Can you really blame them, though?

During the War of the Ring, Saruman pushes deeper and deeper into Fangorn forest, cutting down its trees and using the timber for the gears of war and industry. After a time—far too long, if you ask most "hasty" people—the Ents push back, finally flooding everything around Orthanc, thus putting an end to Saruman's ecological reign of terror.

But even Old Man Willow and the Old Forest have, in their eyes, a right to not think too highly of the generally eco-oriented Hobbits, and to even lash out at them, given their history of violence toward *each other*.[1]

So, allow me to rephrase something: Nature isn't malicious in the way we typically think. Rather, nature's response to our actions, though perceived as malice, is really just how cause and effect work.

I believe this is a large part of what Tolkien is hinting at with the inclusion of the Ents (a race accidentally created by the Professor).[2] They are Fangorn forest's response to an attempted genocide. And yes, I'm calling Saruman's deforestation a genocide because that's exactly what it is, if you view trees the way Tolkien did.

Here he is, talking about his love of all things that grow:

> I am (obviously) much in love with plants and above all trees, and always have been; and I find human maltreatment of them as hard to bear as some find ill-treatment of animals.[3]

So, when Saruman attempts to fell the entire forest, it's no wonder the Ents fight back. Tolkien can't bear to watch the Wizard's misdeeds, in the same way most of us couldn't stand to watch a pack of puppies being harmed. Moreover, in Letter #163 Tolkien even admits that he, "longed to devise a setting in which the trees might really march to war..."[4] Saruman's advance on the forest gives the Professor just that!

Fast forward to today, and I'd have to guess the Ents, though far from hasty, are once again primed and ready for war, if they haven't already begun. Humanity has simply pushed too deep into the forests, and for too long, as evidenced by a growing body of evidence.

First off—and I know some of my more conservative readers will scoff at this—but human-exacerbated climate change is *real*, and it has ill effects. Part of the reason for climate change is our insistence on capitalistically consuming resources from our forests faster than they can replenish themselves. Case in point: the idiotic decision to bulldoze sections of the Amazon jungle to make room for football stadiums that ended up hosting less than five matches. Sorry, but if you don't think behavior like this has any lasting effects, then I've got some oceanfront property in Kansas I'm willing to sell you.

Second, a number of diseases have come, and will continue to come from the forests in which we have no business playing God (i.e., seeing them as a natural resource to colonize, consume, and conquer). COVID-19 burst into the scene in 2019, and that was bad enough, but what virus will come next? Who knows what's lurking deep in the heart of the world's most diverse forests? Let alone under the permafrost that is quickly becoming neither "perma" nor "frost." We continue to press on, so at some point the planet will have no choice but to respond in the way all living organisms respond... by defending itself.

My growing fear is that Entish warnings have been sounding off for too long, and, whether we like it or not, open war is inevitable, if not already here. Call me a pessimist, but I don't see how we turn a ship this size quickly enough to miss a collision. We should have turned a long time ago, but we didn't. I mean, we still have fellow humans hellbent on not even acknowledging that we have had any impact on the globe, so forget even turning. We're not even at the wheel half of the time.

And yet, as long as we're still here, I suppose we have some hope, even if our mere existence balances on a knife's edge. Because until we are six feet deep in the ground, there is always hope. I'm just afraid of the degree of suffering that will occur in the meantime. Things are poised to get much worse before they get better, just as the Ents have been warning for some time.

Yours.

---

1. Sometime during the Third Age, trees from the Old Forest would attack the Hedge that protects Buckland, and in retaliation, Hobbits from that region would go on to burn hundreds of trees. During the time of Frodo, the Bonfire Glade (as it's now called) remains a largely open and empty space, save for some brambles and thistles.

2. See Letter #163.

3. Tolkien, *The Letters of J.R.R. Tolkien*, Letter #165.

4. Ibid., Letter #163.

Seven

ON VALINOR & THE AFTERLIFE

> *"Are the Ring-bearers who travel to the Undying Lands after the events of* The Lord of the Rings *granted immortality, or is it just a stopping point on their way to the grave? Is this similar to the Christian idea of receiving a reward for one's faith?"*

— Tim Higgins

Dear Tim,

No one really knows what happens to mortals after they die in Middle-earth, nor are we sure what happens to any of the Ring-bearers after their time in Valinor. However, there is one peculiar thing we can be certain of: death is seen as a gift of Ilúvatar,[1] which seems to imply there is *something* beyond not only Middle-earth but even the Undying Lands.

Among some Elves, it is believed that after Men (and Hobbits) die, their souls (*fëar*) gather in the Halls of Mandos[2] before departing to a place unknown to even the Valar. Whether that happens years or even decades after the Ring-bearers' arrival in Valinor is anyone's guess. In *Akallabêth*, it is said that those who voyage to the Blessed Realm, "wither and grow weary the sooner, as moths in a light too strong and steadfast,"[3] but how long that might take is unknown. Once it does happen, it can be assumed they, too, will pass into the great beyond like all other mortals.

Again, what this existence is *like* is beyond all comprehension. Ilúvatar surely knows, but all our writings can impart nothing more than mere speculation. One such speculative text is "Athrabeth Finrod ah Andreth," which features a dialogue and debate between an Elf called Finrod and a human woman called Andreth. After a lengthy back and forth, Finrod says the following:

> "That is one thing that Men call hope [...] Amdir we call it, 'looking up.' But there is another which is founded deeper. Estel we call it, that is 'trust.' It is not defeated by the ways of the world, for it does not come from experience, but from our nature and first being. If we are indeed the Eruhin, the Children of the One, then He will not suffer Himself to be deprived of His own, not by any Enemy, not even by ourselves. This is the last foundation of Estel, which we keep even when we contemplate the End: of all His designs the issue must be for His Children's joy."[4]

To the heart and mind of a universalist such as myself, that last line stands out. "When we contemplate the End," says Finrod, we trust that the joy of *all* God's children will be considered. In a world full of great evil, this is a bold statement. But like the earliest Christians who were by and large also universalists, Elves have a strikingly devout belief in the combined power and goodness of their God—the One God—Eru, and his power to bring bliss to *all* people.

With that said, is this like the Christian belief that God only rewards those who do his will? It depends on what you mean by that question. In an age where the Christian faith has, in so many absurd ways, been hijacked by abominations such as the prosperity gospel, it's hard to read "Christianity" and "reward" in the same sentence. But I think I understand you: Is passage to Valinor a reward for their dedication to the Quest?

I don't believe so. Rather, it seems that admittance to the Undying Lands is granted so that the Ring-bearers can find peace and rest. The Ring is a great evil, and bearing it for any time whatsoever—even as briefly as Sam possesses it—is quite possibly the worst thing that could happen to anyone. It's a special type of risk, and with it comes a "privilege" reserved for no other non-Elf.

Again, I don't see this as a reward, but more an act of pity and mercy for having to bear something with as much malice as Sauron's Ring. Now, what happens *after* moving on from Valinor—whether Ring-bearers are further rewarded for their efforts—would fall into the category of conjecture, and not something I could even begin to take a guess at.

In ruminating over all of this, though, I do wonder if Sam ever gets to see Frodo again. In Appendix B to *The Lord of the Rings*, we learn that after his wife Rosie dies, Sam leaves Bag End, entrusts his daughter Elanor with the *Red Book*, and sails to the Undying Lands, presumably to see his friend once more. That is, if Frodo is still alive. A lot of time has passed—over sixty years, in fact—and Frodo's wounds are profound. Valinor assuredly extends his life, but to what degree? While I hope they get to reunite after all those years, perhaps sharing stories over pints of ale—assuming they still come in pints!—no one can be for certain.

In the end, however, if the tales are true, then Eru is both good and powerful enough to secure for us all, including Frodo and Sam, a blissful end, in the land beyond whatever lies past the Halls of Mandos.

Yours.

---

1. From "Of the Beginning of Days," in *Quenta Silmarillion*.

2. The Halls of Mandos lie on the northern shores of Valinor.

3. Tolkien, *The Silmarillion*, 316.

4. Tolkien, *The History of Middle-earth X: Morgoth's Ring*, "Athrabeth Finrod Ah Andreth."

Eight

ON ALLEGORY

"Throughout The Lord of the Rings, *I have noticed a commonality between the protagonists and Christ. Frodo, an innocent Hobbit, bears the burden of the Ring—which seems to represent evil and corruption—to the bitter end. Gandalf sacrifices his own life so that others can escape Moria. Later, he returns more powerful than before. What, then, are Tolkien's religious or spiritual beliefs and are Christian analogies only apparent in* The Lord of the Rings, *or are they also evident in his other writings?"*

— **Sharon Wohnoutka**

Dear Mom,

While there are commonalities between many of the characters from Tolkien's tales and the figure of Jesus from the New Testament,

The Lord of the Rings has to be considered "pre-Christian," drawing from Anglo-Saxon, Finish, Norse, Germanic, and Celtic sources like Beowulf, the Kalevala, and the Poetic Edda,[1] rather than the Bible. As you correctly point out, however, portions of Frodo's story do indeed resemble Jesus bearing the Roman cross in and through Jerusalem; and yes, Gandalf returns from the dead a la the Risen Christ; but themes such as these precede Christianity, just as Middle-earth precedes the time of Jesus.

C.S. Lewis' *The Chronicles of Narnia*, on the other hand, doesn't. It can't. Allegories need to come after the thing they point to, and Aslan most assuredly points directly to Christ. I don't think Lewis was ever attempting to hide his intent, especially given how he makes it clear that the Pevensie children live in 1940s London, nearly two millennia *after* Jesus, making it a decidedly Christian piece of literature.

In *The Lord of the Rings*, however, there is no single "Christ figure." Instead, while every principal character possesses traits and undergoes certain experiences paralleling what we read about in the Bible, they are done so archetypically, not analogously. In other words, Christian themes can be found scattered all throughout Tolkien's Legendarium, but they are only Christian because these themes are *universal*, not the other way around.

Frodo, for instance, follows the pattern of the child scapegoat,[2] as well as the suffering servant,[3] just as Jesus did. But when Mr. Baggins leaves Middle-earth for the Undying Lands, it is because he continues to become ill, never able to fully find rest back at home. This suggests no direct parallel to Jesus' ascension narrative, outside of the fact that both leave their friends for an unknown heavenly realm. Their reasons for doing so are verifiably incongruent.

Gandalf, too, leaves for Valinor aboard the White Ship, but not before dying and resurrecting during the events of the War of the Ring. In your question, you refer to this act as a sacrifice, and in many ways, that's what it is. *I* know what you mean—that Gandalf gives up *his own life* to save his friends—but "sacrifice" is a loaded term, and I must assert that too much of Christian atonement theology is imbued with archaically-oriented sacrificial language. In other words, we have this image of a broken and beaten Son, taking on the Father's wrath that was meant for us, every time we hear "Christian" and "sacrifice" in the same sentence, which you will never find in Tolkien's writings.

You *are* right, though; both Gandalf and Jesus die and resurrect, altered but the same. They each return more powerful—if power is even the correct term—but "fully realized" is probably a better way of putting it.

The parallels are obvious.

And yet, death and resurrection are themes also predating Christianity. Jesus is hardly the first godlike figure to die and rise back to life, even if Gandalf is the first and only Istari to do so.[4] The point being, parallels in thematic elements do not an analogy make. As world-altering myths—and let's be clear, that's what both *The Lord of the Rings* and the Bible are—they each "steer us towards the true harbor."[5] But that's just how universal truths go; one need not be an allegory for the other.

As a good mythologist, Tolkien understands this, which is why he doesn't let his Catholicism cloud his ability to create such a profound mythology. Lewis, in my opinion, cheapens *his* story by being too on the nose—he doesn't even change Peter's name, for goodness' sake!—but Tolkien had no such constraints, and thus, built the more interesting world, one essentially devoid of out-and-out allegories.

On the other hand, I would be remiss not to also mention how Tolkien himself describes *The Lord of the Rings* as a "fundamentally religious and Catholic work; unconsciously so at first, but consciously in the revision."[6] But again, sharing thematic Christian elements and being an allegory are two vastly different things. Not for nothing, but for something to be "catholic"—in the vaguest sense of the world—is for it to be "universal," "through the whole," or "all inclusive." This is what I've been saying all along: the truths contained within *The Lord of the Rings*—indeed, all of Tolkien's Legendarium—are Christian in the sense that they are universal. Love. Self-sacrifice. Empathy. Pity. Compassion. Patience. Kindness. Fellowship. Friendship. All of these are Christian truths, but none of them are exclusive to the Christian faith. They are catholic—that is, "through the whole" of all faiths.

Is this what Tolkien meant by "Catholic?" I believe it is. In Letter #142, he goes on to talk about how he deliberately refrained from referencing religion at all, and that all the themes from his Catholic faith became imbued in the story and the symbolism almost by accident.

But can't we expect this from all myths that "steer us towards the true harbor?" They tap into the truths of the universe, regardless of the religious language that becomes affiliated with them. Frodo—or Aragorn and Gandalf for that matter—need not be an allegory for Christ for us to draw great wisdom from the text. As the *universal* Logos,[7] Christ is in all our favorite Middle-earth heroes, but none are allegories for Jesus. Incidentally, none of the stories' villains are allegories for the devil either. Remember that for Tolkien, the Logos is universal—"catholic"—which means even Gollum and Sauron possess the spark of divinity. (If you're ever up for a challenge, read *The Silmarillion*; you'll find that what I'm saying is backed up in the text—everything that is, and was, and will be, comes from the One, Eru Ilúvatar.)

At the end of the day, *The Lord of the Rings* is indeed a religious text, though it makes very little mention of religion at all. But in writing it this way, I believe Tolkien is able to convey even greater truths than, say, Lewis does with "Narnia." Sure, *The Lion, the Witch, and the Wardrobe* is a perfectly fine book as far as the story goes, but it will always remain hamstrung, relying on another text for its cues. Tolkien's books, on the other hand, are able to tap in directly to the truths of the universe without the need for a mediator, and as such, end up standing toe to toe with all the other great mythologies humanity creates.

Your Son.

---

1. https://tolkienaboutscifi.wordpress.com/2017/07/11/christian-and-pagan-myth-in-lotr/.

2. Lynn Whitaker's essay, "Frodo as the Scapegoat Child of Middle-earth," does a wonderful job explaining this archetypal character arc.

3. Isaiah 53.

4. The Istari are the Order of Wizards, a title assigned to five Maiar sent to Middle-earth during the Third Age.

5. Rather than being a direct quote, this is more likely a synopsis of something Tolkien said, purported initially by long-time friend, C.S. Lewis. It is part of a longer conversation between the two (as well as Hugo Dyson) that took place on September 19, 1931.

6. Tolkien, *The Letters of J.R.R. Tolkien*, Letter #142.

7. Logos is commonly translated as "Word" in John's Gospel, but the concept has very little to do with actual words. In Greek philosophy, the Logos was that which held the universe together, the "structuring principle of reality," as it's been called.

Nine

ON CHANGE

"The world is changing: I feel it in the water, I feel it in the earth, and I smell it in the air. How would you describe both the individual and group development throughout The Lord of the Rings?*"*

— Guy Miller

Dear Guy,

Nothing forces change like traumatic life circumstances. Just ask Frodo Baggins. The pierce from the Morgul blade, the sting from Shelob, and especially the burden of the Ring, forever change him, so much so that after the events of *The Lord of the Rings,* Frodo can no longer endure the pain of growing old in the Shire, and so he leaves for the Undying Lands, never to return to Middle-earth.

But trauma needs not be the only catalyst for change. Sometimes all that's needed is to step outside our borders and come into contact with people who are not like us. That's what happens to the four Hobbits who leave the Shire in TA 3018, as they meet Men both evil (Bill Ferny) and noble (Faramir), Elves from various realms (Mirkwood, Rivendell, and Lothlórien), Dwarves from under the mountains (Gimli and Glóin), and even Ents (Treebeard). Through these encounters, they become Hobbits who are able to drop their biases in exchange for curiosity and, eventually, wisdom.

For instance, after Frodo wakes from his coma in "the last homely house east of the Sea," he admits the following to Gandalf:

> "I have become very fond of Strider. Well, fond is not the right word. I mean he is dear to me; though he is strange, and grim at times. In fact, he reminds me often of you. I didn't know that any of the Big People were like that. I thought, well, that they were just big, and rather stupid: kind and stupid like Butterbur; or stupid and wicked like Bill Ferny. But then we don't know much about Men in the Shire, except perhaps Breelanders."[1]

In *The Wisdom of Hobbits*, I use this example to illustrate how we are so often like Frodo, on one hand admitting we know nothing of a given situation, yet making strong assumptions nonetheless. That's why we all need a Gandalf in our lives: "you don't know much even about them," he says, "if you think old Butterbur is stupid [...] he is wise enough on his own ground."[2]

So, *where does Frodo's assumption come from? Why assume "Big People" are stupid?*

Because that's a part of the cultural milieu of the Shire.

We get a glimpse of this prejudice at the very opening of *The Fellowship of the Ring*. In a lengthy exchange between Old Noakes of Bywater, Daddy Twofoot, and the Gaffer, all three Hobbits hardly mince words. Bucklanders are called "queer," meaning they live on the "wrong side" of the Brandywine River. Brandy Hall is even derogatorily referred to as "a regular warren, by all accounts."[3] The fascinating thing about this insular worldview is that Bucklanders live a mere fifty miles from Bywater and Hobbiton, so it's not like they are very far, off in some distant corner of the wilds. This goes to show just how narrow-minded some of the Hobbits of the Shire truly are.

For Hobbits like Old Noakes or Daddy Twofoot to ever change, they would have to meet and befriend at least one Bucklander. Then, in any instance where that old timey prejudice would start welling up in them, forcing out xenophobic sentiments, they would at least have to check themselves and acknowledge that their descriptions couldn't be used on *all the Bucklanders.*

This type of acknowledgement is, according to contact hypothesis,[4] a main catalyst to change. When we come into contact with people groups different from our own, empathy and compassion overtake suspicion and mistrust—not all the time, but frequently enough that we have to take notice of the phenomenon.

All manners of change take place throughout Tolkien's Legendarium, however—for good *and* for ill. When the Fellowship loses Gandalf at the Bridge of Khazad-dûm, for instance, the group dynamic shifts. A darkness falls over them, and cheery moments become more and more infrequent. Individually, change happens for all involved, subtly for some individuals, but more profoundly for others. For example, as Boromir snaps out of a near trancelike state in his attempt to overtake Frodo at Amon Hen, he instantly ascertains just how deceptively powerful the Ring is. For Aragorn, growth tends toward being more gradual, intensifying alongside the events of the War of the Ring (though his wisdom with regards to the Ring can't be understated). But in the end, change comes, and when it does, there is almost nothing anyone can do to stop it.

Such a reality is part of the sadness of life. The Elves attempt to put an end to change, and in doing so, fall for the trap of "nostalgic regret," as Tolkien has put it.[5] Though they don't typically taste death, the Elves' plight also strips them of a portion of their life, which is sadness unto itself. Hobbits and Men, on the other hand, experience change, and change is hard. Frodo is forever transformed, which makes the ending to his story quite bittersweet indeed—we'll never see him in the Shire again! Those who aren't afforded passage to the Undying Lands also bear with them a level of sadness, not only because they have to watch their friend leave, but for the unavoidable reality that everyone dies in the end (except Sam, who also gains passage west after his wife Rosie passes away). As the gifted songwriter Lin-Manuel Miranda once penned, "death doesn't discriminate;" it takes indiscriminately.

But death is also a gift in Middle-earth. In fact, it is *the* Gift of Ilúvatar himself, as it allows anyone who tastes it to go beyond the boundaries of Arda, beyond the bounds of even the Music of the Ainur. So, in a way, change is predestined in Tolkien's world, just as it is predestined in ours. How we go about changing, however, and when we decide to choose such a fate, are up to us. Frodo chooses to answer the call to adventure, just as his uncle Bilbo did fifty years prior. Merry, Sam, Pippin, and even Fatty Bolger make the same choice, and in doing so, all bind themselves to the inevitability of change. And for that, as fanatics of Tolkien's Legendarium, we are grateful.

The question then becomes: will *we* also embrace change?

Yours.

---

1. Tolkien, *The Fellowship of the Ring*, 247.

2. Ibid.

3. Ibid., 24.

4. In psychology, contact hypothesis argues that prejudice can be reduced between majority and minority group members by placing folks in appropriately close proximity.

5. See Letter #197.

Ten

On Plato's Ring

"I am not aware that J.R.R. Tolkien consciously patterned the One Ring after the Ring of Gyges, but many scholars have seen connections between the two. Apart from the obvious similarities of granting the wearer invisibility, how does Plato's story of the Ring shed light on why Hobbits were the ideal Ring-bearers?"

— **Gary Michelberger**

Dear Gary,

When I decided to compile this collection of letters in this way—where my friends and readers essentially become coauthors—this was the kind of question I had in mind, the one I never saw coming. What an exciting and thought-provoking challenge your question poses!

You're right, though: there is *no evidence* Tolkien patterned the One Ring after Plato's Ring of Gyges, though there are indeed superficial similarities, perhaps even a smattering of deep-seeded ones. But before we get into a comparison between the two rings, let's first introduce the latter for those not familiar.

In Plato's *Republic*, Glaucon uses the myth of a shepherd in the service of the King of Lydia who discovers a magical ring on a corpse in a crater where he tends sheep. After putting the ring on his finger, with the setting facing inward, the shepherd becomes invisible, which leads him to seduce the Queen, kill the King, and take over the kingdom.

In this story, we are led to believe that prior to coming into contact with the ring, the shepherd is a good man, but after, with all consequences put on hold by the magic of the ring, Gyges becomes a killer driven by power.

The point of the myth is obvious: Plato is exploring whether we, as self-identified Manichean "good guys," are really as good as we'd like to think. When immorality doesn't lead to obvious negative consequences, what will *we* do?

For Plato, Gyges is the cautionary response—we will kill to consolidate our own power.

In Tolkien's world, things are fairly different. For starters, while in his story Plato seems to be suggesting that *anyone*, no matter how virtuous, moral, and upright will fall prey to the ring, Tolkien adds more nuance and depth in his writing. In essence, Plato's analysis of the person is limited by its binary structure—before the ring = good; after the ring = bad—while Tolkien's view is that all characters fall on an ever-changing and evolving spectrum.

Where the two views intersect, however, is in the character of Boromir. The man of Gondor is the most like Gyges in that his desire for power consumes his mind, to the point of betraying the friends he vows to protect. And though Boromir finds redemption in defending Merry and Pippin before succumbing to Saruman's onrushing orcs, it is only after the One Ring has been lost to him. Should Boromir have been successful in taking it from Frodo at Amon Hen, his soul would have been lost, and the Quest failed.

Boromir is just one character, however, and doesn't represent the broad range of responses to the Ring found in Tolkien's tales. Galadriel and Gandalf, for example, resist the Ring and its powerful lure, even though either could have personally justified its use with their good intentions. But the former gives up all her current power and dominion to reject the Ring. Here's how Tolkien describes the dramatic scene at the Mirror:

> She lifted up her hand and from the ring that she wore there issued a great light that illumined her alone and left all else dark. She stood before Frodo seeming now tall beyond measurement, and beautiful beyond enduring, terrible and worshipful. Then she let her hand fall, and the light faded, and suddenly she laughed again, and lo! she was shrunken: a slender elf-woman, clad in simple white, whose gentle voice was soft and sad.[1]

From here, Galadriel announces that she has passed the test and will diminish into the West, renouncing her own power in the name of goodness itself.

But even when our favorite Middle-earth heroes *are* deceived by the Ring, as Frodo is at the Cracks of Doom, it is after a great struggle—mental, physical, and even spiritual. This critical moment for Frodo doesn't prove Plato's assertion that people merely refrain from immorality out of fear of getting caught. In fact, quite the opposite is true. Frodo literally drives himself to the point of death to destroy this Ring, and even though it gets the best of him in the end, its reasons for doing so are far removed from Plato's starkly binary assessment.[2]

Frodo's resilience, combined with a love of friends and fellowship greater than a love of power, is what makes the humble Hobbit the best bearer of the Ring. And while even the noblest of Hobbits can and will capitulate to its lure, Tolkien's myth teaches us that our choices still matter. We can still possess the Ring, and do good, even if its temporary victory over us is inevitable.

Had Frodo—or most Hobbits for that matter—been in Gyges' place and found Plato's ring, I feel as though the myth would have fallen in on itself for the sole reason that Frodo would have just gone back to tending the sheep, perhaps only using the ring to occasionally steal mushrooms from Farmer Maggot's crop, or play pranks on his uncle Bilbo. To imagine Frodo seducing Arwen, killing Aragorn, and taking over the reunited kingdoms of Gondor and Arnor, seems better suited to a quirky piece of fan fiction than a true and honest look at how Middle-earth operates. (But before anyone gets the idea to create such a work, just remember that Tolkien's writings don't go into the public domain for quite some time, and the Tolkien estate doesn't mess around with stuff like this. So, best to keep such fantastical writing to yourself and your closest of friends.)

Until our next meeting, take care of yourself. And if you find any magic rings laying around, please be careful with them!

Yours.

---

1. Tolkien, *The Fellowship of the Ring*, 410.

2. For more on my analysis of Frodo and the Ring, see chapters 4 and 5 of *The Wisdom of Hobbits*, and Part IV of *Mimetic Theory & Middle-earth*.

Eleven

ON ECOLOGY

*"Given there are multiple idyllic ecosystems in
Middle-earth—the Shire, Rivendell, Lothlórien—did
J.R.R. Tolkien believe that these locales should translate
from the realm of fantasy to the human world?"*

— **Dillon Naber Cruz**

Dear Dillon,

Each of the three locations you mentioned are enchanting for different reasons. Rivendell represents both, "the last homely place east of the Sea"[1] and the epitome of Elven "magic" (though they themselves would never use such a term). In Lothlórien, time operates differently than anywhere else in Arda, and the seasons of change fail to penetrate her borders. Then there's the Shire: humble, down to earth, and open to all the ebbs and flows of change (seasonally more so than culturally).

As beautiful as Rivendell and Lothlórien are—both my wife and daughter have consistently chosen Rivendell as their favorite place to imagine living in all of Middle-earth—the Shire is the only location of the three that would (somewhat) translate from the realm of fantasy to the human world.

Allow me to explain.

In Letter #197, Tolkien says the following of the Elven race:

> [Elves] wanted to have their cake and eat it: to live in the moral historical Middle-earth because they had grown fond of it (and perhaps because they there had the advantages of a superior caste), and so tried to stop its change and history, stop its growth, keep it as a pleasaunce, even largely a desert, where they could be "artists"—and they were overburdened with sadness and nostalgic regret.[2]

Magical as they are, both Rivendell and Lothlórien fall for the same trap. They have become sanctuaries against evil, but in doing so, have also become ensnared by their own nostalgia. In Lothlórien, for example, nothing seems to change like elsewhere; not the seasons, not the weather, nothing. For more than a thousand years, time has passed without decay under the golden branches of the Mallorn trees. And while this lack of decay ensconces the land, creating a nearly timeless piece of art, like all things that fail to change or grow, it's beauty eventually fades.

By the Fourth Age, we witness this decline with the Elves. Just as the prophesies foretell, after the Rings of Power are rendered null and void by the destruction of the One Ring, they fade into the West, leaving their former homes to also diminish.

The Hobbits, on the other hand, welcome the changing of the seasons (though they probably aren't too keen on experiencing yet another Fell Winter[3]). In spring, they prepare their soil and plant seeds in the ground. Summer brings harvest, and then festivals to celebrate them. Autumn is a time for baking, jarring, jamming, and preparing for winter, when most trees and shrubs go dormant, and Hobbits try to stay warm by the fire. Then spring rolls around and the folks of the Shire do it all over again.

This is the natural pattern of the world, and nothing escapes it—not even Lórien! Sure, the Elven realm remains unblemished for thousands of years, but even this place can't escape the laws of entropy. The Elves fade, and so too does their land.

So, what lessons are to be learned from these idyllic places? Two initially come to mind:

First, we must learn to adapt to change and embrace death. Those Brandywine tomatoes you love so much... they *will* die, no matter how much you fight it. The wiser among us realize this, which is why they simply accept the inevitability of death and adjust. Sure, the plant will die, along with all the fruit on its vines, but did you know there are at least two ways to see it come back to life the next year, even when it's technically categorized as an annual? *As a permaculturist, of course you do!* You either bring the plant back the traditional way by harvesting the seeds, drying them, etc. etc., or the natural way, by letting the spoiled fruit continue to rot in the soil, thereby leading to volunteer plants the next spring. I've used, and continue to use both methods, and each are magical.

Second, we will never get rid of evil by hiding from it. While the lands of Lothlórien and Rivendell have become synonymous with escaping from the ills of the world, they do nothing in actively solving its problems. Here's the thing, though: folks from the Shire generally don't do anything either. That's what makes extraordinary Hobbits like Frodo, Sam, Merry, and Pippin so... well... *extraordinary*. They step outside their cultural norm to actually care about the ills of the world and learn how they can help solve them, even though they realize they are, for all intents and purposes, ill-equipped.

As to the ecosystem of the Shire... yes, I believe Tolkien intentionally created it as a model for how we can live in harmony with the world around us (I say as much all throughout chapter 3 of *The Wisdom of Hobbits*, as well as chapter 11 of *Mimetic Theory & Middle-earth*). In fact, I also readily admit, in conversation with friends and in writing, how I have modeled our farm after what I read in the Prologue to *The Lord of the Rings*. On our farmland in Northern California, we enjoy peace, quiet, and good tilled earth. From the garden, vineyard, and orchard, we create plain and obvious artisanal goods: salsas, sauces, jellies, jams, and wines. Our hens give us eggs, which we use in all sorts of hobbity ways. And when the seasons come and go—and with those changes the death of our crops and animals—we adapt, adjust, and continue to press on, just as Hobbits have done for centuries.

As one in all but size, I am happy to continue this legacy the Hobbits have created, and believe the more of us that do, the better our world will be. I know you'd agree with me, especially given your affinity for permaculture and sustainability.

Until next time.

Yours.

1. Tolkien, *The Fellowship of the Ring*, 252.

2. Tolkien, *The Letters of J.R.R. Tolkien*, Letter #197.

3. The Fell Winter was a bitter, cold, and long-lasting winter during 2911–12 of the Third Age that caused food shortages all throughout the Shire.

Twelve

ON CLASS STRUCTURES

*"The Shire, like the current world, uses a class system.
And yet, there doesn't seem to be a whole lot of tension or
animosity between Hobbit classes. Is there anything we can
learn about the Shire's relationships between the different
classes? If so, what can we then apply in our own world?"*

— **Tabby Asbury**

Dear Tabby,

As you probably know, my belief is that there is plenty of wisdom to be found in the charming, rustic people of the Shire. Though they indeed live within the confines of a class structure (as you point out in your question), the relationships between the classes typically remains respectful and cordial, more so than observed in most societies.

And yet, Hobbits can also be myopic and guarded (to a fault). Such prejudices are generally reserved for folks outside their geographic borders though, not necessarily *within* their close societal structures.[1] For instance, at the very onset of *The Fellowship of the Ring*, we witness a full-on gossip session between a few of the Rustics[2] at *The Ivy Bush*, wherein they proceed to make up all sorts of stories and throw out underdeveloped opinions of Bucklanders living a mere fifty miles away. One could argue that in behaving this way, they are besmirching the more Educated Gentlehobbits[3] of East March, but they are not doing so *because* they are Educated—there are Hobbiton locals like Frodo and Bilbo who are among the informal aristocracy. The Rustics of *The Ivy Bush* gossip about the Bucklanders because "those Hobbits" are simply "other"—Hobbits just outside the bounds of the Shire, Hobbits to be kept at a distance.

Within geographic communities, however, classes seem to get along quite nicely, and that is in part because the civic authority of the so-called aristocracy expresses their duties mildly: "in the administration of the Shire, rather than the wielding of power."[4] As I state in *Mimetic Theory & Middle-earth,* Hobbits,

> Desire simple pleasures (of which there are plenty) over piles of gold (of which there aren't many). In doing this, they create a culture where stewardship is valued above possession. That is simply to say, according to the customs of the Shire, tending to something is viewed more favorably than owning it.[5]

Evidence of this comes from long after the events of the War of the Ring, when Sam Gamgee, the epitome of what it means to be a Rustic, is affectionately given the surname "Gardner" as a token of the Shire's appreciation for his life and dedicated service to beautifying their land. He becomes a Master at this revered profession and ends up going down in history as one of the most accomplished Hobbits of all time.

In our modern world, hoarded gold is valued more than simple gardens and certainly prized over nights full of food and cheer. Just look at who the *really* rich are, and how the system is set up to keep them rich. It's not your favorite artist or athlete on top—though they are all doing just fine—it's executives and owners who have the *real* money and power. And what do so many of them do? Hoard their riches in offshore bank accounts in tax-friendly countries. Meanwhile, though business owners like Daniel Ek are worth \$3.6 billion—with a "B"—Spotify only pays artists between \$0.003–\$0.005 per stream.

How generous!

My solution? I should wish for folks like Mr. Ek to read *The Wisdom of Hobbits,* for if he did, and if he took everything to heart, I bet he would realize \$3.6 billion—again, with a "B"—is a *bit* excessive. But I'm also a pessimist, because I'd be remiss to not mention the power and lure of the Ring is perhaps even more powerful than that of my prose.

What a shame.

Not everyone is Daniel Ek, however. And so, in the meantime, what people like you and I can do is continue to fight for the working class among us, so that the gap between the haves and the have nots shrinks, while the number of those who *have* grows. There's no reason a CEO should make five-hundred times as much as the regular Joe of the company, and I'm confident every humble yet honorable Hobbit would agree with me.

Yours.

---

1. I will note, however, that Bilbo Baggins counters this example, but not because he is in a different societal class than the Rustics (see my next note for a definition). It is for the sole reason that Bilbo gets mixed up with "outsiders" like Gandalf and the Dwarves.

2. The Rustics, as David Rowe points out, are the "salt-of-the-earth Hobbits who make up the majority of the population." They include "farmers, tradesmen (such as ropers, millers, and smiths), and others whose skill is primarily with their hands." (Rowe, *The Proverbs of Middle-earth*, 5).

3. Rowe goes on to describe the Gentlehobbits as the "great or wealthy families who make up an informal Hobbit aristocracy." (Ibid.)

4. Ibid.

5. Distefano, *Mimetic Theory & Middle-earth*, 171.

Thirteen

ON DIVINE INTERVENTION

"There are key moments when an outside will or force makes small nudges for good: Bilbo finding the Ring, Frodo and Sam finding water in Mordor, etc. Then there is the grand intervention of sending Gandalf back after he dies. So, why does Ilúvatar and the Valar intervene in the way they do (in The Lord of the Rings *specifically, which is very different from how they intervene in* The Silmarillion*)? Do they have a limitation in power, an obedient constraint, or something else?"*

— **Michael Raburn**

Dear Michael,

When it comes to mythologies of any kind—whether from Tolkien's Legendarium or the Bible—no writer is bias-free regarding God or theology. Moreover, being that Tolkien is *not* the author of the original book that makes up *The Lord of the Rings* but is instead offering an English translation of an *ancient book*, originally written by Bilbo Baggins, and then added to by Frodo, Merry, Pippin, and others, we are getting lots of opinions from lots of people (mainly Hobbits) about how certain events during the Third Age play out. In other words, like all firsthand accounts, the original book (called the *Red Book of Westmarch*), inevitably contains *some* biases. How could it not? In the same way, *The Hobbit* is partial toward a very *specific* Hobbit, namely the author of the story, Bilbo himself—I'm not the only one who thinks it's *possible* he fudged certain details of his encounter with the spiders in Mirkwood, am I?[1]

To that end, given how Tolkien's Legendarium is all a part of the same lore, I have to assume what I do about all tales such as this: different voices have different opinions, and as history progresses, these opinions will shift and even distort. Further, as far as myths go, we rarely know their true (generally oral) origins; meaning, we don't even know who these original voices truly are. Case in point: *The Silmarillion*.

The book that we currently have—the one written in English by Tolkien—is at one point translated into Westron by Bilbo, using texts by Rúmil, Pengolodh, and other Elves. Rúmil, a lore master of the Noldor, is alleged by some to have written Ainulindalë (the first part of *The Silmarillion*), while a Second Age unknown author perhaps wrote Valaquenta (the second part). The third part of the book, Quenta Silmarillion, is probably written by Pengolodh.

Now, back to the heart of your question.

Perhaps the answer comes down to perception. Every culture has grids and filters their stories pass through. Elves are no different. Neither are Hobbits. But Elves and Hobbits are as different as the west is from the east, which means their stories will be, too. Not just their stories, though; everything about them will be different. They will have different theologies, different philosophies, different cosmologies, different ethics, politics, rituals... everything.

So, is it any wonder why Eru and his divine council seem to behave a certain way during the First and Second Age texts, yet another in the Third Age and beyond? On the one hand, you have Elven lore masters compiling texts based on *their* traditions about who God is, what God is like, whether God is good or not, how God created the world, why there is evil and suffering throughout Arda, and so on. On the other hand, you have humble Hobbits with no noticeable religious lineage, telling stories and emphasizing the things that are important to *them*—stepping out onto the Road to adventure away from a life surrounded by "peace and quiet and good tilled earth."[2]

Two different contexts, two different perceptions, and thus, two different ways of telling their stories.

But again, this is how we would expect a mythology to read. In fact, it's exactly how the Bible reads. Though God may be the same "yesterday, today, and forever,"[3] there are many theologies represented between the books of Genesis and Revelation. As the old joke goes, if you get two rabbis discussing the scriptures, you'll come away with three interpretations of them.

The fact of the matter is, no sacred text has ever dropped out of the sky and onto the shelves of Christian bookstores, nor have the words in any book come from the pen of Ilúvatar himself. But rather than this being a disheartening fact, these various perceptions present an exciting opportunity to have interesting discussions about important works of literature that have helped shape humanity for a very long time, and lends freedom to speculate over the very questions you have posed. Because that's all we can do—speculate. These are heavy hitters—theodicy, the problem of evil, why a good God doesn't step in and "do something"—and no amount of philosophizing will ever give a satisfactory answer. All we can do is trust that Eru is good, and that in the end, the Music of the Ainur will resolve its melody.

Yours

---

1. After all, Bilbo has a history of fibbing about how certain events play out during the events of *The Hobbit* (i.e., how he comes upon the One Ring).

2. Tolkien, *The Fellowship of the Ring*, 1.

3. See Hebrews 13.8. Even on this concept, however, the Bible is quite unclear. All throughout the Scriptures, God is said to change his mind (Exodus 32:14), have regret (Genesis 6:7), and reward those who say no to him when his actions don't line up with his alleged character (see Matthew J. Korpman's book *Saying No to God* for a detailed look at this fascinating biblical phenomenon).

Fourteen

On Eucatastrophe

"J.R.R. Tolkien describes eucatastrophe as a 'sudden glimpse of Truth,' where joy and sorrow become one. He drew parallels to the Gospels' portrayal of the birth and resurrection of Christ as the 'greatest' true fairy-stories. How do you envision the concept of eucatastrophe offering glimpses of Truth in today's world? And considering the evolution of societal values and symbols, do you think the concept of Truth has changed?"

— **Nora Sophia**

Dear Nora,

I see eucatastrophe all around me. Or at least I tell myself that's what I'm seeing. As humans, it's difficult to distinguish between what we are objectively witnessing and what we are wanting to observe. As a Tolkien-head, I know that eucatastrophe breaks into Middle-earth quite often; so, *I want it to happen* in my world, too. That's kind of how mimetic theory works, if you catch my meaning.

That said, I also *just can't help* but notice sudden glimpses of truth breaking into our world, pulling us toward the same type of hope Tolkien introduced throughout his many tales. In a sometimes-hopeless world, it can admittedly be difficult to think of examples of these eucatastrophic events, but they *are* littered all over the place.

In early 2024, for example, two days after notifying my employer that I would be resigning from my social services position, they terminated me. I had never had a write-up, never had a negative performance evaluation, never even had a verbal warning for any action in all my years of employment. And still, I was fired—when I thought I had six weeks left of work. In most instances, this would be a terrible situation to be in. But because of how California labor laws work, I became entitled to unemployment benefits, which held my family over until I was able to substitute teach on a more regular basis. Further, leaning into the eucatastrophic elements, I used this opportunity to invest time into my publishing company that I hadn't been able to while employed as a social worker. And in doing so, I helped grow the company to a position where I no longer need an employer, let alone one as retributive and petty as my former agency.

Of course, the skeptic would say in a world full of billions of people, coincidences that end in a net positive are bound to occur, and with no more likelihood than those ending in a net negative. Fair enough. Overall, however, I can't help but hold to a worldview where some kind of force is either pushing, pulling, dragging—I don't care which—humanity toward something of a happy ending, where justice is in fact *for all*, where suffering ceases to be, and where love is the anchor and glue of all interdividualistic relationships. Because that's the key element of any good fairy tale—the happy ending. Things can't end in tragedy, for God's sake. The hopelessness would be too much to bear.

As we progress toward this happy ending, there will be bumps along the way. There will also be cultural shifts that emphasize some aspects of humanity while de-emphasizing others. Yet, behind the subtleties of culture and all the idiosyncrasies that come with its ever-evolving nature, transcendent truths will remain. We often equate the transcendentals with medieval scholasticism (primarily St. Aquinas), but the "first principles" of Truth (Thought and Logic), Beauty (Aesthetic and Artistic), and Goodness (Morals and Action) go all the way back to Aristotle. And no matter how often we see our current cultural climate shifts, these principles weave themselves through the whole of it all. As they do, it will be our job as creative beings to document the journey so society can continue to progress past the point of our current collective consciousness.

One such piece of literature that does this can be found in a most unusual place—on the PlayStation 5, in an apocalyptic universe where a mutated fungus has upended all normal life. I am of course talking about *The Last of Us*.

In a 2024 paper for The Tolkien Society's *Vingilot,* entitled, "A Tale of Two Scapegoats: Comparing and Contrasting the Surrogate Victimage of Frodo Baggins and Ellie Williams," I explore the many ways in which the beloved video-game series has succeeded in tapping into some of the deepest truths of the universe, first and foremost what it means to live a very real, *very* messy human existence. And though *The Last of Us: Part II* leaves us wondering if there will in fact be a hopeful culmination in the yet-to-be-released *Part III*, there are eucatastrophic elements scattered throughout which leave me cautiously optimistic for something positive to come amidst the deeply traumatic story, first of which would be Ellie's redemption.

But back to Tolkien.

No matter how far removed we get from *him* and *his* cultural place in history, the truths contained within his Legendarium remain. Again, that's just the nature of Truth—with a capital "T," as you put it—that no matter how much subjectivity our cultures abound in, there are objective truths weaving their way throughout all good literature (and video games), and will continue to do so into the future. It's like timeless music from folks like Otis Redding, Sam Cooke, and Miles Davis—it doesn't matter if it's 1950 or 2050, their tunes will still be relevant. So, too, will *The Hobbit*, *The Lord of the Rings*, and all the Professor's other works. In fact, it seems he just gets more and more popular the further removed from his life we get.

So, evolving societal values? Of course! Evolving symbols to represent those values? No doubt! But always remember that there are truths—or, Truth, if you prefer—that weave their way throughout every concept and symbol human societies can create.

Yours.

Fifteen

ON THE PROBLEM OF SUFFERING

"Many people have joked that despite J.R.R. Tolkien's incredible world-building ability, that given the world he created, couldn't Sauron have been handily defeated by enlisting the Eagles to take the One Ring straight to Mt. Doom for its destruction? This is Tolkien's 'problem of evil and suffering.' Why make everyone suffer pain, war, and loss, when the evil could have been dispatched directly?"

— **Dave Montoya**

Dear Dave,

To quote the Professor: "shut up."

Yours, Matthew J...

I'm kidding!

Well, I'm not kidding that this was Tolkien's response to the short-form version of your question.[1] And look, maybe the Eagles *should have* been commissioned to help. Or at least such an option *should have* been considered. Maybe that's what Gandalf meant by, "Fly, you fools!" Like, literally, fly to Mordor, you idiots!

I'm not convinced, though, given that one of the greatest strengths of the Fellowship's plan is its stealth. Nevertheless, your question brings up a good point, and one more pertinent to our shared philosophical inclinations: *if* the solution to the problem of evil is simple, why would a good God continue to allow its existence?

First off, I don't personally believe that Eru Ilúvatar can simply *will* something into happening, regardless of what any Elven writer says. That's not how I see the One—God, the Force, whatever you call such an entity—moving in *our* world, let alone Middle-earth. And let's not forget, everything we read about in the pages of *The Lord of the Rings*, *The Hobbit*, and other Tolkien lore, is a direct reflection of the Music of the Ainur, which of course includes the grating dissonance (i.e., evil) of Melkor. This is unavoidable.

So, am I saying that God *can't* prevent evil and suffering?

Yes... and no.

Yes, in the sense that God is not all-powerful, as the Calvinists would have us believe. (And if God *is* all-powerful, then God is not what we can call good, so let's not even go there.)

But no, the One *is* fully capable of working in tandem with—Tolkien uses the word "his," but I prefer "their"—creation to stop evil.

Let's be clear: helping to stop evil is Gandalf's entire role and function. As an Istari, he is sent as an emissary by the Divine. But he has limited "power," if you will. He is not to overstep human volition, but is to act as a guide, a sherpa—both literally, while atop Caradhras, and figuratively, as a wise philosopher-type—so the Free People of Middle-earth are nudged toward restoration and reconciliation through the elimination of evil and suffering.

So, truth be told, the Eagles... Gandalf... it doesn't matter. Ilúvatar, though perhaps directing both Eagle and Wizard to a degree, can only work within the bounds of the world he himself has created. In Middle-earth, volition is respected (sometimes to a fault). I often hear the term "free will," but this is a loaded and charged concept. Eru certainly gives his children some semblance of autonomy; though, as I argue in my first two "Tolkien books," all fall on a spectrum. In other words, human freedom is not a cut and dried, binary type of situation. Many wills are enslaved to many different vices—like golden rings—Gollum perhaps being first among them.

On the other hand, to be truly free in Tolkien's world—Tom Bombadil comes to mind—is to not really have the choice between good and evil, because the choice is in fact crystal clear. Evil is an absurdity, as ridiculous as the Ring holding any sway over the Master of the Wood. Tom does what Tom does, without taking on any outside models, and that is a quality no other character can claim.

As free as Tom is, however, he would be insufferable as a direct associate of the Quest. As Gandalf reminds the Council of Elrond, Tom would likely put the Ring down or forget it somewhere, given its unimportance to him. So, maybe freedom of will isn't the end-all-be-all some claim it to be. Gandalf certainly has the freedom to choose the good, and yet he has something Tom doesn't—the ability to see the importance of the Quest, and the desire to aid the children of Ilúvatar in making their world a better one, full of goodness, justice, and love. Tom, on the other hand, seems to be too self-absorbed to care about anything outside the immediate borders of the woods.

Again, though, Gandalf is hamstrung by the rules of the universe. Eru is, too. That's just how relationality goes. Within relationships, there is room for distance, for hurt, for pain, for heartache, for grief, for mourning. So, even if the One *could* prevent all these less-desirable aspects of existence, perhaps the relationships within such a world would be stale, cardboard cutouts of the real thing. There would be no growth, no room for "I'm sorry" and "I forgive you." Nothing hard-earned, nothing real.

In fact, could it not be argued that without evil, there'd be no great works of literature? Hobbits would essentially be reduced to writing books about the art of growing and smoking pipe-weed (not a bad thing to be known for), but they would not be adept storytellers. There would be no story to tell, no hero's journey, no overcoming great odds.

Do I say this to cheapen anyone's suffering? Of course not! Like Gandalf, Aragorn, and all decent people (and Wizards) of Middle-earth, I want to see an end of suffering. But I also realize that the moral arc of the universe is a long one. So, in the meantime, my belief is that we might as well get some really good stories out of our situation. Because sometimes, that's the only thing that gets us through all the pain.

Yours.

1. As Dave points out in a personal correspondence on January 15, 2024, "It's almost like he's a comedian responding to someone asking him to explain a joke. "No, I will *not* explain the joke, because if I explain it, I will ruin it. If you don't get it, there's nothing I can do to 'make it funny' for you. An explanation won't do."

Sixteen

On Good & Evil

*"I read somewhere that within J.R.R. Tolkien's stories,
good actions generally end with good outcomes, but evil
actions with evil intent can also end up producing good (i.e.,
rushing the armies of Mordor north to the gate to crush the
army of the West, clearing the way for Frodo and Sam). I
assume good actions plus evil motives, or vice versa, would
lead to evil results. I wonder: did Tolkien see evidence of his
principle in the world around him?"*

— Jim Wehde

Dear Jim,

Tolkien's world is a monotheistic one, though the degree to which
Ilúvatar intervenes can be disputed. Where all Tolkien scholars agree,
however, is that the One indeed influences the narrative toward a *good*

ending, but is also tempered by human (and Hobbit) volition. Hence, the history of the world plays out toward an end goal, but it's often a case of one step forward, two steps back (given humanity's propensity toward evil).

Whether this means the "principle" behind how we get to the best outcome would look as in your question is a matter of conjecture, because so much of what takes place in our favorite stories involve an intertwined dance of both good *and* evil, so much so that it's often impossible to distinguish between the two.

For instance, you could say, "Sam had *good* intentions (protecting Frodo) in treating Gollum *evilly*, and so unpredictably such actions led to an *evil* result (Gollum never finding redemption)." But a quick retort could be, "Because Gollum never finds redemption, he pursues Frodo and Sam to the Cracks of Doom, and in doing so, accidentally destroys the Ring (something Frodo *fails* to do)." And could we *not* call this an overall "good?"

And yet, it's hard to label the destruction of one of the Children of Ilúvatar as "good." It's also dubious to say all of Sam's behavior toward Gollum is fully justified and thus "good" (though we all empathetically understand his leeriness toward the creature). But to say that the ends justify his means is an ethical stretch I'm not willing to take.

This interconnected dance between good and evil does not mean the former condones the latter, however. In fact, the truth is quite the opposite. Because Eru is good, and because he has some type of "power"—though it does seem quite tempered in places—there is always a pull toward a good end. In other words, the goodness of Ilúvatar moves the narrative toward a good end despite an immense degree of evil suffered over the course of the story.[1]

Is there evidence of this tension between good and evil in our world? It depends on one's worldview. I happen to believe there is a force we can call God moving in the world, drawing all people toward himself, and that given enough time, God will achieve such a goal. I'm not certain whether Tolkien would affirm such a belief, though some of his characters do.

But again, does goodness only come from: good actions + good intention, or evil actions + evil intent? I would hesitate to be so reductive. In Middle-earth, as well as in our modern world, God seems to move in mysterious ways and can find even the most hidden cracks through which to pour out grace and love. I fear such a principle would only diminish God's ability to move in the world.

I would be curious if you disagree with me here. Perhaps I am missing something, or that there is more of a pattern that I am not aware of. But sometimes patterns can trick us and exist as nothing more than random events woven haphazardly together. So, I hesitate to affirm such a principle, even if Tolkien intended for there to be one.

Yours.

---

1. I put forth similar thoughts in my letter to Nora Sophia, entitled "On Eucatastrophe."

Seventeen

ON MINDFULNESS

*"I have been learning about the importance of mindfulness
and being present for the moment I am in. What can
Middle-earth teach us about presence, mindfulness, and
living in the now?"*

— **Crystal Kuld**

Dear Crystal,

Just about everything. Of course, that's what good fiction does. It forces readers to be present with the story, especially when we're talking about a work like *The Lord of the Rings*. Every page is imbued with such meticulous detail that it is impossible to quickly breeze through the pages. When you read Tolkien, you have to slow down and take your time, because if you don't, you'll be certain to miss something important along the way.

For Middle-earth specifically, much insight can be gleaned regarding mindfulness. Tolkien must have been intentional in including the concept of living in the now in the way he used prose to slowly guide readers through every twist and turn along the path of "there and back again." The pages beg us to sit down and stay a while—slowly drawing pipe-weed into your lungs as you sit under the willow tree and smell nasturtians' scent dancing across the breeze. (And before you break out your red pen, yes, I meant *nasturtians*. I know it's technically *nasturtiums* these days, but take that up with Tolkien.[1])

Mindfulness, at its heart, is about attention. And Tolkien demands yours—not through gimmicks, but through reverence. We don't merely watch Frodo and Sam *pass through* Ithilien. We walk every step with them. We smell the stewing herbs and conies—sans po-ta-toes—feel the ache in their feet, and hear the rustle of dry leaves under tired heels. And in that stillness, that presence, something sacred happens.

You see it with the Ents. Treebeard doesn't hurry along his way or interrupt those he's in conversation with. He listens the way an old tree listens—with patience and wisdom grown over the ages. And you certainly see it with the secular Hobbits, who somehow make the act of gardening feel like a spiritual practice. And it is. At least, it is for me.

At Happy Woods Farm, I do my best to live like a Hobbit. I garden, tend to the chickens, smoke my pipe, and generally take my time. There's no rushing the tomatoes. You water, wait, weed, and wait some more. Presence is not a concept for me. It's a posture. It's how I move through the day, listening to the soil and watching the bees work the lavender. (And every so often, yelling at the dog for digging up a newly planted blueberry. But that's another letter for another friend.[2])

Middle-earth reminds us, again and again, that life happens not in the grand moments, but in the small ones. Sam looking up at a single star in Mordor. Frodo resting in the house of Tom Bombadil. Merry and Pippin drinking Ent-draught. These aren't side notes; they *are* the notes. These moments are the melodies of mindfulness playing soft and low, and Tolkien knew how to listen.

I think the Shire is our best model for mindfulness and living in the now. It's a place where time is measured in meals, not milestones or meeting deadlines, where people show up not to conquer but to cultivate. I try to live that way, not to escape the world but to live more deeply in it. The sacred is not found somewhere else—it's in the pipe smoke, in the fresh eggs, in the clucking of hens, in the warmth of good tilled earth between your fingers and even under your nails.

So yes, mindfulness is everywhere in Middle-earth. You just have to slow down long enough to notice it. And if you ever forget what that looks like, come visit me. I'll be out in the garden with my pipe, watching the clouds drift by, trying to remember how to spell *nasturtians.*

Yours.

---

1. As I note in *The Wisdom of Hobbits,* for those who aren't aware, the nasturtian was the subject of a disagreement between Tolkien and a proofreader for *The Fellowship of the Ring.* This poor fellow corrected Professor Tolkien's "nasturtian" to its now more commonly spelled "nasturtium," apparently not realizing that the nasturtium is a type of watercress, while the nasturtian is a popular garden flower found in Bag End. With its read, orange, and gold flowers, it was and still is a favorite among gardeners. Needless to say, the correction was redacted, and Tolkien's preferred spelling now appears in the text.

2. He knows of whom I speak.

Eighteen

On Meaning

"*If you had to reduce everything J.R.R. Tolkien wrote down to make it mean only one thing, what would it be? And do you think he meant for his books to be approached like this?*"

— Laci Bean

Dear Laci,

Certainly not! When we talk about a story having one meaning, we have entered the realm of allegory. Think about C.S Lewis' *The Lion, the Witch, and the Wardrobe* for a second. In that tale, the name Aslan is synonymous with Christ. In essence, Aslan *means* Christ. There are other meanings we can draw from the totality of the text, but the insistent allegory hamstrings it in very key ways.

In *The Lord of the Rings,* as well as many other tales from Middle-earth, there is no such limitation. Instead, Tolkien's stories exist as stand-alone myths. As such, I contend that meaning can be found in nearly infinite ways, just as it is with life.

When people ask, "Matt, what do you think the meaning of life is?" I tend to answer, "There is none." If they can get past the shock of such a statement, and gather up the courage to ask for clarification, I often go on to say something like the following:

> If there were one meaning to life, then meaning would be limited. But in having no meaning, it opens up the possibility for infinite meaning. Go find what it means to you. I'll figure out what it means to me. And maybe we can report back and see what overlaps and what doesn't.

Of course, I'm not suggesting we play fast and loose with our interpretation of Tolkien (or other mythologies, for that matter). In approaching any sacred text—yes, I'm calling *The Lord of the Rings* a sacred text—we must be respectful of the lore from the world in which it originates.

At the same time, if in reading Tolkien, we are truly dealing with a mythology—and I believe we are—there is nothing stopping us from taking a creative hermeneutical approach to the works. As a Girardian, I can admit my biases in seeing mimetic theory in *all* my favorite literature. I can further admit that Tolkien, while he didn't have humanity's imitative nature in mind when he wrote his books, indeed spun a story that lends itself to a strong Girardian analysis (which I've tackled in *Mimetic Theory & Middle-earth*).

Again, though, we are dealing with a tale so well-put-together, there are *many meanings*, not just one. In *The Wisdom of Hobbits*, I make it clear that my biggest personal take away from *The Lord of the Rings* is that the deepest truths of the universe can be found in the most unlikely places—in the Shire, among simple Hobbits living on simple land. In that book's follow-up, I was frequently much more pessimistic, which is no surprise, given we were talking about the Ring and the perverted desire it represents.

But these are the meanings *I* get from the text. Just as it is with books like the Bible, we are all going to bring our own grids and filters and life experiences to the stories. A feminist, for instance, is assuredly going to focus on characters like Éowyn and Galadriel,[1] while scholars like Tom Emanuel have argued in favor of Tolkien being a liberation theologian.[2] Philologists, on the other hand, might say that everything comes down to language, given Tolkien was, first and foremost, a linguist.[3]

The point—and perhaps I'm repeating myself here—is that there are infinite meanings we can glean from any works such as Tolkien's. So long as we respect the world from which the texts derive, and the lore that comes with them, we should have freedom to explore all the many themes and motifs the Professor both wittingly and unwittingly brought to the forefront of the minds of so many fans.

Yours.

---

1. I address the potential feminism of Tolkien in Letter #5 of this collection.

2. See Emanuel, Tom. "J.R.R. Tolkien: Liberation Theologian? Reflections on Teaching Tolkien in a Progressive Christian Context." From PCA 2022 National Conference: Tolkien Studies VIII.

3. In *Splintered Light: Logos and Language in Tolkien's World*, scholar Verlyn Flieger writes that Tolkien's "profession as philologist and his vocation as writer of fantasy/theology overlapped and mutually supported one another," going on to add that, "his scholarly expertise informs his creative work." (Flieger, *Splintered Light*, 5–7).

Nineteen

ON GOD'S RELATIONALITY

"Why is God, or 'Eru,' seemingly so distant from those in Arda? Many Middle-earth denizens know old stories, songs, and bits of wisdom, but what part does Eru play in their day-to-day lives?"

— **Ellen Haroutunian**

Dear Ellen,

Why does God seem so distant in *our* world? If I knew, I'd probably write a book about it and make a lot of money. Then I could hoard it all and guard it like a now-infamous dragon.

Sorry, I lost myself for a moment there...

Perhaps Eru—God—isn't all that distant from anyone in Arda, though. Maybe humans have become so distracted that they've stopped paying attention. Gandalf, for instance, is sent by the divine council[1] to aid humanity in defeating Sauron, and he is largely seen by Shire residents as a nuisance at best and sworn enemy at worst. Hobbit children love him, of course—we've all witnessed the fireworks he brings—but adults are leery. In his own words, he's a "disturber of the peace."[2]

If the halflings only knew...

As to what part Eru plays in the lives of everyday people in Middle-earth... I'm certain it depends on who you ask. Maybe this is becoming too obvious a theme in these letters, but I wholeheartedly believe there can be no consensus on this question. Ask an Elf from Rivendell and you may get one answer, but ask one from Mirkwood and you'll likely hear an entirely different one. While in Michel Delving, my money is on an entirely new idea being introduced, with those in Bree protesting all of it.

Here's a fun thought experiment, though: *I wonder what Orcs think.*

In *The Lord of the Rings*, they serve Sauron, but this can't be an innate impulse; such servitude must be taught. Political allegiances? Religious loyalties? These are learned behaviors, largely mimetic ones. Orcs don't just pop into existence with a political philosophy oriented toward a despot named Sauron. That's not how Orc life works.

So, does Eru work toward *their* redemption? I wonder...

In our world, I firmly believe God works toward the redemption of even the most tyrannical among us—the Bill Fernys and Ted Sandymans of the world. And as a universalist of some kind, I believe God ends up arriving at God's ultimate goal. So, if Eru is anything like our God, my guess is that he's busy doing *something*. Or, maybe I'm totally anthropomorphizing "him." Maybe God is not like that at all.

That's why I prefer the secularism of the Hobbits. Sure, some of them may debate matters of theology from their ivory smials—as if there could be such a thing—but such academic pursuits are not their focus. Life is all about getting their hands dirty and cultivating crops and community.

Hobbits are in no way perfect—they're far too insular and disposed to Luddite-ism—but they certainly understand that the real stuff of life is not found in speculating about the gods. Rather, it's found in being a steward in your community and on your land. That's it. Small stories and tall tales around a fire. Bread with butter and jam. A robust red wine.

So, distant? Maybe Eru isn't distant at all. Maybe God is found in the little things of life. That's been my experience. Have you tasted bacon and mushrooms? If that's not heaven, I don't know what is.

God is found in the bacon and the mushroom, believe me!

The Buddhists would probably track with what I'm saying here, and I believe you will, too. Only in having a theology that places God "out there" do we experience the distance of God. When we turn inward, however, to our own communal and interdividualistic selves, we start to realize that God is everything and everything is God. That includes you. That includes me. That includes the bee and the butterfly, the asparagus and the aubergine, the lion and the lamb, the sheep and the goats.

My guess is that some who walk through Middle-earth would see Eru in the same light, while others would deem my musings as heresy. Hobbits would have likely checked out three paragraphs ago after all that talk of food. And that's why I love them. In all their secularism, they can't help but experience God in just about everything they do. They just wouldn't have the language for it.

Yours.

---

1. Known as the Valar.

2. Tolkien, *The Fellowship of the Ring*, 44.

Twenty

ON WORLD BUILDING

*"J.R.R. Tolkien has been called the Writer of Worlds ...
is there anything that you would change about any of the
worlds he created? Between* The Hobbit *and* The Lord of
the Rings, *which world do you like most and why?"*

— **Desimber Rose**

Dear Desimber,

The Hobbit and *The Lord of the Rings* both exist in the same world.
Same maps, same mountains, same pipe-weed. But whereas *The Hobbit*
is told from the hand of Bilbo—curious, flustered, fussy, and entirely
loveable—*The Lord of the Rings* is passed down and carried by Frodo,
Sam, Merry, Pippin, and the rest. And their voices, shaped by war and
loss, tell a different kind of tale.

That's the beauty of Tolkien as a mythologist. He didn't just write stories, he built a mythology, layered and living, told and retold through different lenses and literary textures. *The Hobbit* is lighter, a bedtime story told to Hobbits in their tweens. *The Lord of the Rings* is more like an epic song sung by the fire after a great sorrow. It's not that the world has changed, only that the storyteller has.

Now, as a writer, I prefer the prose of *The Lord of the Rings*—its gravity, its cadence, its depth. There's something sacred in its slow-moving pace. The significance of the story weighs more, and its language carries that weight. But as a Hobbit in all but size, I'd be lying if I didn't tell you my heart will always beat strongest for the Shire.

The Shire is where the good things grow.

It's where gardens bloom in curved rows along stone walkways, where backyards spill over with pumpkins, berries, and marigolds. It's where hens cluck contentedly in the yard, and roosters wake the valley long before any sleepy Hobbit is ready to be woken. There's a rhythm to the Shire that feels more like music than anything else. Things are done when they need doing—not a moment sooner, but certainly not a moment later either. People show up with gifts of fresh bread just because. Doors are rarely locked. Neighbors wave, not to be polite, but because they mean it. Well, mostly. The Sackville-Baggins don't, but let's not dampen the mood by bringing them up!

But yes, there's always time for a pipe and a pint.

I try to emulate this pastoral way of living in my own life as best I can. At our acreage in Northern California—Happy Woods Farm—we cultivate the same sort of slow magic. The chickens are content. The gardens are tended. Tomatoes, blackberries, wine grapes, peppers, onions, garlic... these are our treasures. We cultivate the earth, not to conquer it, but to be in relationship with it, to understand it, to listen to it. That's something Hobbits understand, and it's something most modern people have forgotten.

When I smoke from my pipe, it's not to look whimsical or wise. It's to be still. To breathe. To remember that nothing truly sacred ever comes from rushing or being rushed. When I plant tomatoes, I think about Samwise and his box of Galadriel's earth. I think about what it means to restore things after they've been broken. When I sit near the fire with Michael, sharing a drink or watching the wind move through the trees, I feel closer to whatever people mean when they say "God." Because if there is a divine presence that lives anywhere, I'm convinced it's found in the soil, in the strawberries, and in the sound of chickens scratching through the mulch.

That's why I say the Shire isn't just my favorite place in Tolkien's world. It's my *model* for life. Not Minas Tirith. Not Lothlórien. Certainly not Mordor. *The Shire.* Because while everyone else is chasing dragons or drawing swords, the Hobbits are hosting dinner parties, preserving peaches, and discussing the finer points of pruning tomatoes. And somehow, by doing all these seemingly small things, they end up saving the world.

So, would I change anything about Tolkien's world? Maybe. Perhaps I'd nudge him gently toward including more women in the story. A bit more diversity wouldn't hurt, either. But to change Middle-earth in any major way would feel sacrilegious. Not because it's perfect, but because it's mythic. It meets us where we are. It grows with us, evolves as we evolve, and teaches us, over and over again, that the smallest voices often carry the greatest truths.

And between *The Lord of the Rings* and *The Hobbit*, which world do I prefer? They're both the same, really. Just told by different Hobbits at different stages of their lives. But which *place* do I prefer? The Shire, without question. And as long as I have breath in my lungs and dirt under my fingernails, I'll continue doing my best to live like I belong there. Because I do. We all do.

Yours.

Twenty-One

ON HOBBIT WISDOM

"If your average Hobbit wrote a self-help book, what life advice would it offer?"

— Stuart Delony

Dear Stuart,

If your average Hobbit were to write a self-help book—and I say "average" not pejoratively, but as high praise—it would not contain seven habits of highly effective anything. Nor would it claim to teach you how to manifest your desires using some universal law that may or may not be thinly veiled capitalism in wizard's robes. No, a Hobbit's guide to life would look quite different. It would likely be shorter, almost certainly bound in something soft and leathery, and most definitely smudged with bacon grease and smelling of pipe-weed.

But make no mistake: *its wisdom would be real.*

First, there'd be something about breakfast. And second breakfast. And elevenses. Any Hobbit worth their weight understands that life is best measured in meals, not in meeting deadlines. A good day begins with buttered toast, includes at least two teatimes, and ends with a pipe under the stars. If you're anxious, you're probably hungry. If you're angry, you probably skipped lunch. And if you're overwhelmed, well, perhaps you're just trying to do too much before second lunch (do they have that?).

You'd then be instructed, gently, of course, to go outside. Not to "exercise" in the way Men do, all of them grunting and sweating in front of each other, but to walk. Slowly. Barefoot, if you're brave.[1] Because a Hobbit knows that healing happens one step at a time, preferably among the cabbages and sunflowers.

There'd be a chapter on gardening, not for productivity's sake, but because tending to a plant is a way of tending to oneself. You'd learn that weeding a patch of strawberries can be a kind of prayer, that composting is a metaphor for transformation, and that mushrooms are a gift from Eru, even if you have to beat any number of young Hobbits to them.

Further along, there'd be advice on friendship. How to recognize a good one (they bring you food and drink without asking). How to be one (listen more than you talk, and always split the last piece of toast). And how, in the end, it's your friends who carry you up the mountain, or down from it, depending on your need.

A Hobbit's self-help book would not rush you toward greatness. It would not urge you to "conquer your goals" or "crush your obstacles." Instead, it might suggest a nap. A long one. Under a tree, preferably.

Because, after all, change takes time, and so does recovery. And if the world insists on rushing, a Hobbit will kindly insist on resting.

Toward the back, in slightly crooked handwriting, you'd find one final piece of advice: Never underestimate the small things. A hot meal. A warm fire. A friend's laughter. A bit of pipe-weed at dusk. A rustic windmill perfectly placed between the garden and the vineyard. These are not distractions from life. They *are* life. The world may chase dragons and gold, but a Hobbit will always choose the comfort of home, and in doing so, find the real treasure.

My pitch for this book would be as follows: if you're tired of striving, if your soul feels frayed, if you've forgotten what it's like to feel the earth between your toes, I recommend the *Hobbit's Guide to Life*. It won't make you famous. It won't make you rich. But it will make you whole.

Yours.

---

1. I once walked Maui's Pipiwai Trail barefoot. It is a 2-mile hike known for its lush bamboo forest and stunning Waimoku Falls.

Twenty-Two

ON THE BODHISATTVA

"Despite not taking place in our timeline, would you consider Gandalf to be a bodhisattva?"

— **Michael Machuga**

Dear Michael,

Leave it to you to ask a question that makes me want to light my pipe, pour a glass of something warm, and sit by the fire until the stars come out. Which, let's be honest, is historically how most of our conversations have gone. Whether it's by text, at the bonfire, or in that hypothetical future where we live on the same street, your questions always stir up the good stuff.

So, to your question...

Well, first of all, yes.

And second of all, hell yes!

But let's take a slow stroll to get there.

From a purely ontological standpoint, Gandalf is different from us. He's a Maia, after all, one of the lesser Ainur, sent by the Valar to assist the Free People of Middle-earth in resisting Sauron's power. He's not born of Arda in the same way Hobbits or Men are. So, in terms of origins, Gandalf is more like an angel than a human.

But the point of your question isn't about metaphysics, it's to inquire about mission, purpose, and the orientation of being. And in that regard, Gandalf fits the bodhisattva mold perfectly.

You know this already, but for the readers who haven't read *The Bonfire Sessions*: a bodhisattva is one who, though capable of attaining liberation, chooses to remain in the world to help others achieve theirs. They forsake final enlightenment not out of reluctance but out of love, compassion, and fellowship.

Sound familiar?

Gandalf *could* have returned to the West. He certainly had enough excuses. After the Balrog dragged him into the depths of Moria, he could've said, "You know what, I tried. Let the Elves sort this out." But he didn't. He came back as Gandalf the White not to rule, not to seek power, but to guide and to support. To whisper just enough into people's hearts to help them choose *the good* for themselves.

Gandalf chooses humility over power time and time again. He could have taken the Ring—Frodo tries to offload it on him—but he refuses. Not because he fears the Ring would *fail* in his hands, but because he knows it will *work*. That's the danger Boromir fails to recognize when he tries to take hold of the Ring at Amon Hen. But Gandalf knows true power doesn't look like domination, it looks like encouragement and companionship, like showing up to the bonfire with good pipe-weed and sitting beside someone until they feel strong enough to face the darkness on their own terms.

That's precisely Gandalf's mission: to aid in preserving the freedom of the Free People of Middle-earth and to create conditions where they can grow, choose, stumble, and rise again. That's what makes him different from, say, Saruman. Saruman wants control. Gandalf wants growth. And any good bodhisattva knows the difference.

Now, of course, because of our mimetic nature, none of this would matter if we didn't also believe that *all of us* carry the potential to become bodhisattvas. You don't need to be a Maia to help someone see the light. You don't need a staff and robes to sit with someone in grief or remind them they are loved. In fact, I think Gandalf would argue that some of the greatest bodhisattvas are the ones who don't even know that's who they are. Think of Samwise. Think of Frodo. Think of you; whether you accept such terms or not, every time you're there for me when I need an ear, a friend, and a smoke.

So yes, Gandalf is a bodhisattva. But so is *anyone* who helps guide others toward liberation without needing to be the hero of the story. Anyone who sacrifices comfort to keep another from falling into despair. Anyone who chooses to stay, not because they must, but because they *love to.*

And you are one of those people, if not first among them.

Yours Always.

A RESPONSE TO JOSH
SCOTT OF TOLKIEN LORE

Dear Josh,

Thank you for taking the time to review *The Wisdom of Hobbits*. I was genuinely grateful for your engagement with the book, and I've listened carefully to your critiques, especially your concern about authors injecting politics into their readings of Tolkien. On the surface, I actually agree with you—there's something frustrating about someone trying to force Tolkien's work into narrow ideological categories, or worse, reducing it to a mere vehicle for modern partisan agendas. That kind of reading flattens a rich mythological landscape into little more than a talking point, and none of us want that.

That said, I do want to offer gentle pushback on one specific point—the belief that engaging with climate change in the context of Tolkien's work is necessarily "political," at least in the partisan sense of the word.

Climate change, as I understand and address it, is not a matter for party lines. It's not a red state or blue state issue. It's not about blaming or shaming. It's about survival. It's about stewardship. It's about living wisely within our ecological limits. In that sense, climate change is *political* only in the broadest sense of the word, that is, as an issue concerning *the polis*, the whole community. And frankly, reading *any* book—especially in an age of book banning, censorship, and rising ideological division—is an inherently political act. To read, and read broadly, is to care about truth, perspective, and presence in a world that often resists those very things.

Now, to be absolutely clear, I am *not* suggesting that Tolkien had climate change in mind as he wrote his beautiful mythology. That would be a strange and anachronistic claim. *The Wisdom of Hobbits* doesn't argue that Saruman's destruction of Fangorn is an allegory for global warming, or that the Scouring of the Shire is a coded warning about carbon emissions. But as I see it, the beauty of myth is its ability to speak truth forward into generations far beyond its time. Tolkien may not have had the scientific language of climate models or greenhouse gases, but he *did* understand what happens when we push too deeply into the forest. He *did* see what becomes lost when the machine of industrialization tears through the slow, sacred rhythms of the natural world.

When Saruman turns to mechanized destruction in Isengard and Fangorn, we are shown a vision of progress untethered from wisdom.[1] When the Shire is taken over by Sharkey and his cronies—chopping down trees, blackening the skies, turning Hobbit-holes into drab and joyless cells—we see the effects of industrial greed and ecological disregard. What follows? Smoke. Dust. Felled trees. These are not just aesthetic changes; they are warnings.

From a modern scientific perspective, we now understand that these exact actions—deforestation, pollution, relentless capitalistic development—are primary drivers of anthropogenic climate change. Tolkien didn't write a textbook on climate science, but he *did* offer a prophetic glimpse into the repercussions of losing our reverence for the natural world. And that's where I believe a reader today, grounded in both scientific understanding *and* mythic imagination, can draw meaningful parallels not as allegory, but as a form of moral and ecological wisdom.

If anything, my hope in writing about these issues is not to politicize Tolkien, but to universalize the invitation he offers his readers. To live more like Hobbits. To slow down. To cherish the green and growing things. To remember that progress without restraint often leads us to ruin, and that the cure for such folly may be found in second breakfasts, in quiet gardens, and in the good tilled earth beneath our furry feet.

So, while I understand your concern for a partisan politicization of Tolkien, I'd gently suggest that recognizing climate change through Tolkien's lens is not an imposition onto the text, but a reflection of its deeper truths. Truths that, like all good myths, grow alongside us and speak anew in every age.

Yours.

---

1. Tolkien, *The Two Towers*, 75–76.

A RESPONSE TO DR. CURTIS GRUENLER

Dear Dr. Gruenler,

Thank you so much, Dr. Gruenler, for your thoughtful and generous review of *Mimetic Theory & Middle-earth*. Your closing statement truly resonates with me, and I find it heartening that you acknowledge the potential for future discussions around the intersection of Girard's theory and Tolkien's work. Here's what you said:

> Distefano has made good music from the resonances between Tolkien and Girard. There are more songs to be sung, and I'm sure Distefano would welcome the singers around his fire with a cup of their favorite equivalent of Old Winyards.[1]

As you correctly noted, this book is not meant to be the final word on Tolkien and Girard; rather, it's an invitation for further exploration and conversation. *Mimetic Theory & Middle-earth* is the first of its kind, and while it builds upon the foundation laid by Hayden Head's insightful essay, "Imitative Desire in Tolkien's Mythology: A Girardian Perspective," it's also deeply personal. The aspects of Girard's theory I chose to emphasize were those I felt were most relevant to the intricate relationship between mimetic desire and the moral framework within Tolkien's Middle-earth.

As you know, Tolkien's world is vast and multilayered, and applying Girard's theory of mimetic desire to this mythology is an endeavor that will certainly take more than one voice to thoroughly explore. As you rightly put it, there are more songs to be sung, and I am confident that I won't be the only one to sing them. I envision *Mimetic Theory & Middle-earth* as a launching pad—a starting point for others to dig deeper, develop new insights, and perhaps challenge some of the interpretations I've proposed. I welcome that intellectual collaboration and anticipate that future scholars, writers, and thinkers will come to see and expand upon the resonances between Girard's work and Tolkien's world in ways that I haven't even considered.

I hope that others who pick up this thread will feel encouraged to join the conversation, much like a fellowship gathering around the fire with whatever it is they put in *their* pipes. The work that remains to be done, especially when it comes to integrating Girard's ideas into the broader narrative of Tolkien's mythos, is as boundless as Middle-earth itself. My hope is that this book will be one step in an ongoing dialogue, one that will continue to evolve with the contributions of many.

What a day it would be to have a society where conversations such as the ones we are having here become commonplace and a mainstay!

Again, I'm deeply grateful for your kind words and the space you've given this project in your review. Thank you for recognizing the potential for more songs to be sung, and I look forward to the future voices that will join in.

Yours.

---

1. Gruenler, "Mimetic Theory & Middle-earth," para. 11.

UPDATES ON HAPPY WOODS FARM

Since the publication of *The Wisdom of Hobbits* and *Mimetic Theory & Middle-earth*, Lyndsay, Speri, Michael, and I have taken another exciting step forward in the journey of Happy Woods Farm. We've purchased the property across the street from our friends, so now between the four of us, we own the entire end of the cul-de-sac. It feels like the beginnings of our own little hobbity kingdom, one that's both grounded in diligent hard work and rooted in the possibilities of what's yet to come.

We've already made some big changes, adding water to the new property, ensuring it's ready for future growth. A greenhouse is now in place, and we've set up twenty-four raised veggie beds and six large beds dedicated to flowers. Between all the sunflowers, zinnias, and nasturtians—is that how you spell it?—the garden is already a visual and aromatic wonderland. This year, we're focusing on planting a mix of veggies like tomatoes, zucchini, pumpkins, peppers, and eggplant, alongside fruits that we already have like strawberries, blackberries, peaches, pears, citrus, and wine grapes. Of course, that's just the beginning of what we've got going, but it gives you a good idea as to the progress in that regard.

In 2026, we're slated to plant between forty and fifty fruit trees on the property, plus eight to ten beds of blueberries. It's going to be a fruit-filled future! And we haven't forgotten about our ever-growing flock of chickens. What started with just six birds has now expanded to ten—we had four little wanderers this very year in my garage before transferring them to the coop.

The firewood pile is still impressive as ever, and the carport has been converted into our very own farmer-cave—because, you know, every farmer needs their own cave. For those long nights or chilly mornings, we've got an outdoor firepit ready to go, complete with a cast-iron Dutch oven for all those future stews and soups. A rose garden is currently being planted, and to top it all off, a eucalyptus tree now graces the new property.

We've also put in lighting in multiple places to make sure the farm shines bright at night, whether it's for an evening stroll or a late-night harvest session. Every little improvement feels like a step toward something bigger, a place that's both a haven and a little community.

All in all, Happy Woods Farm continues to grow, evolve, and bring new joys to our lives. Here's to the next chapter—may it be full of flowers, fruit, fellowship, and firelight.

BIBLIOGRAPHY

Bouchaala, Ghaida. "The Vision of Power Between Tolkien's LOTR and Plato." *Medium*. (March 20, 2022). https://ghaidabouchala.medium.com/the-vision-of-power-between-tolkiens-lotr-and-plato-2238f965c962.

Catanach, Dawn. "The Problem of Éowyn: A Look at Ethics and Values in Middle-earth." *The Grey Book: Online Journals of Middle-earth*. Volume 1, 2005.

Distefano, Matthew J. *Mimetic Theory & Middle-earth: Untangling Desire in Tolkien's Legendarium*. Chico: Quoir, 2024.

———. *The Wisdom of Hobbits: Unearthing Our Humanity at 3 Bagshot Row*. Chico: Quoir, 2023.

Emanuel, Tom. "J.R.R. Tolkien: Liberation Theologian? Reflections on Teaching Tolkien in a Progressive Christian Context." From *PCA 2022 National Conference: Tolkien Studies VIII*.

Flieger, Verlyn. *Splintered Light: Logos and Language in Tolkien's World*. Grand Rapids: Eerdmans, 1983.

Gruenler, Curtis. "Mimetic Theory & Middle-Earth: Untangling Desire in Tolkien's Legendarium by Matthew J. Distefano." In *Mythlore: A Journal of J.R.R. Tolkien, C.S. Lewis, Charles Williams, and Mythopoeic Literature*. Vol. 43: No. 2, Article 23 (April 2025). https://dc.swosu.edu/mythlore/vol43/iss2/23/.

Maddox, Rachel. "Flawed and Formidable: Galadriel, Éowyn, and Tolkien's Inadvertent Feminism." *UReCA: The NCHC Journal of Undergraduate Research and Creative Activity, 2018 Edition*. https://digitalcommons.unl.edu/cgi/viewcontent.cgi?article=1033&context=urecak.

Mertens, Jonas. "Weather in Middle-earth or Tolkien: The Weather Master?" In *Journal of Tolkien Research*, Volume 16, Issue 2, Article 1. (2023). https://scholar.valpo.edu/journaloftolkienresearch/vol16/iss2/1/.

Rowe, David. *The Proverbs of Middle-earth*. Toronto: Oloris, 2016.

Tolkien, J.R.R. "Athrabeth Finrod Ah Andreth." From *The History of Middle-earth: Boxed Set*. New York: William Morrow, 2020.

———."Of Dwarves and Men." From *The Peoples of Middle-earth: The History of Middle-earth*. Edited by Christopher Tolkien. Boston: Houghton Mifflin-Harcourt, 1996.

———. *The Hobbit*. New York: Del Rey, 1996.

———. *The Lord of the Rings: The Fellowship of the Ring*. New York: Ballantine, 1993.

———. *The Lord of the Rings: The Return of the King*. New York: Ballantine, 1993.

———. *The Lord of the Rings. The Two Towers*. New York: Ballantine, 1993.

———. *The Silmarillion*. New York: Ballantine, 1999.

———. *The Letters of J.R.R. Tolkien*. Edited by Humphrey Carpenter. Boston: Houghton-Mifflin-Harcourt, 1981.

Tolkien, J.R.R. and Hostetter, Carl F. *The Nature of Middle-earth*. Edited by Carl F. Hostetter. Boston: Houghton Mifflin Harcourt, 2021.

Tolkien, J.R.R., and Tolkien, Christopher. *Morgoth's Ring*. Edited by Christopher Tolkien. Boston: Houghton Mifflin, 1993.

———. *The Book of Lost Tales, Part I*. Edited by Christopher Tolkien. Boston: Houghton Mifflin, 1983.

———. *The Book of Lost Tales, Part II*. Edited by Christopher Tolkien. Boston: Houghton Mifflin, 1984.

———. *The Lost Road and Other Writings*. Edited by Christopher Tolkien. Boston: Houghton Mifflin, 1986.

———. *Unfinished Tales*. Boston: Houghton Mifflin, 1980.

To contact Matthew J. Distefano
for speaking engagements,
please visit www.quoir.com.

Many Voices. One Message.

quoir.com

Made in United States
Troutdale, OR
09/24/2025

34816596R00079